MAKE
BETTER
DECISIONS

MAKE BETTER DECISIONS

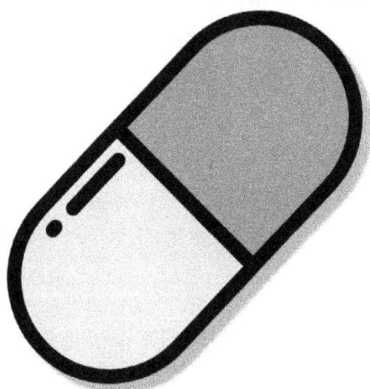

FINDING AND EVALUATING GENERIC AND BRANDED DRUG MARKET ENTRY OPPORTUNITIES

YALI FRIEDMAN, PH.D.
DRUGPATENTWATCH.COM

MAKE BETTER DECISIONS
FINDING AND EVALUATING
GENERIC AND BRANDED DRUG
MARKET ENTRY OPPORTUNITIES
YALI FRIEDMAN, PH.D.

Published in The United States of America
by
Logos Press®, Washington, DC
www.Logos-Press.com
info@Logos-Press.com

10 9 8 7 6 5 4 3 2 1

ISBN-13
Softcover: 978-1-934899-39-7

About this Book

Thanks for reading. If you enjoy this book, please consider leaving an honest review on your favorite bookstore's website. Your feedback helps support the continued development of this book.

Sign up for updates and other news at:
https://www.DrugPatentWatch.com/make-better-decisions/

I welcome your comments, criticisms, and suggestions for additional topics to cover. Please send me your thoughts at admin@DrugPatentWatch.com.

About DrugPatentWatch

DrugPatentWatch is a provider of global business intelligence on biologic and small-molecule drugs, dedicated to helping clients make better decisions.

Critical information on global drug patents is incorporated with litigation intelligence, drug prices, and historic sales figures to help users discover commercial opportunities and forecast future revenue events. Since 2005 DrugPatentWatch has served hundreds of large and small companies in more than 65 countries.

Homepage: https://www.DrugPatentWatch.com
Contact: admin@DrugPatentWatch.com

About the Author

Yali Friedman, Ph.D. is the founder and publisher of Drug-PatentWatch.

Dr. Friedman is also publisher of the *Journal of Commercial Biotechnology* and author of *Building Biotechnology*, which is used as a course text in dozens of biotechnology programs. He was also named one of the 100 most influential people in biotechnology by *Scientific American*.

Dr. Friedman has strong exposure to leading issues in international drug development. Over the span of ten years he developed and maintained the *Scientific American worldVIEW* scorecard, a global biotechnology perspective profiling biotechnology industries and innovation capacity in dozens of countries, and he has been invited to participate in biotechnology industry development forums for international groups such as APEC, in Europe, and throughout Asia.

Disclaimer

This book is intended for educational and informational purposes only. Nothing contained in this book is intended as legal or investing advice.

This book is not a substitute for advice from an attorney. If you require legal or other expert advice you should seek guidance from a suitable and competent attorney or other expert.

Reasonable efforts have been made to ensure the accuracy of this book. However, there may be mistakes or omissions. Further, patents, laws, economic conditions, and their interpretations are constantly changing. Accordingly, this book should only be used as a general guide. It is not appropriate to use this book as an independent source.

Dedication

I am grateful to all the DrugPatentWatch clients I have had the opportunity to serve. I have been privileged to bear witness to the changing needs of stakeholders at the bleeding edge of innovative and generic drug development and healthcare delivery. Thank you all for your questions.

I am also indebted to my very patient wife. She was, in a sense, the first to "read" this book, as she (repeatedly) listened to me describe all the challenges, opportunities, and nuances of drug development and the intricacies of legal and regulatory influences. And, beyond simply passively listening, she has challenged me to dig deeper and to explain better. I thank you, Suzanne, for your patience and for your questions.

Contents

Introduction

This book is the product of more than twenty years of providing guidance to drug development companies and other healthcare stakeholders.

Through developing the first website on the business of biotechnology in the 1990s (now owned by the *New York Times*), editing and publishing the *Journal of Commercial Biotechnology*, and leading data analytics for a subsidiary of *Scientific American*, I have had the fortune of spending considerable time at the bleeding edge of the commercial side of drug development.

The motivation to write *Make Better Decisions* comes from my experiences running DrugPatentWatch, a comprehensive platform to help identify and evaluate opportunities around drug patent expiration and generic entry. In the early 2000s the first version of DrugPatentWatch was developed in response to repeated requests to answer the simple question: "When do drug patents expire?" As the platform matured, it became apparent that there was a strong need for a single source integrating broad strategic guidance to help stakeholders throughout the drug development and delivery value chain. *Make Better Decisions* is written to meet that need.

As with my other publications, the focus of *Make Better Decisions* is on actionable intelligence. Because the legal and regulatory underpinnings of drug development and delivery are complex and change frequently, the approach taken by this book is to explain the current state of affairs and to provide representative examples to help you develop a deep understanding so you can quickly adapt to and capitalize on future events.

A primary objective of this book is to fill gaps in knowledge, helping you leverage your expertise, without being overly exhaustive. I have kept the citations brief and opted to incorporate them in the text rather than as footnotes or endnotes. For readers seeking greater technical depth I have listed some of the books and web-based resources that I found helpful.

Because strategic planning for branded drugs has many similarities to finding and prioritizing generic entry opportunities, this book has relevance for generic and branded companies alike. Likewise, distributors, payers, investors, and myriad other stakeholders will also benefit by understanding the commercial dynamics of pharmaceutical and biotechnology drugs. I hope you enjoy reading the book as much as I did writing it.

Innovative and Follower Drugs

D rugs can be roughly split into two categories based on their technical characteristics, and into two other categories based on their regulatory characteristics.

The two technical categories are pharmaceutical drugs, commonly referred to as small-molecule drugs, and biotechnology drugs, commonly referred to as biologic drugs.

The Food and Drug Administration's (FDA) regulatory framework provides a useful way to distinguish drug types. "New" drugs rely almost exclusively on testing information performed by (or for) the company developing the drug, and follower drugs may either rely entirely on testing performed by others (e.g. generic drugs) or they may rely extensively on testing done for already-approved drugs (e.g. biosimilars).

SMALL-MOLECULE AND BIOLOGIC DRUGS

The most popular, and oldest, technical category of drugs is small-molecule drugs. These drugs, also commonly called pharmaceutical drugs, tend to be orally doseable as tablets, capsules, or liquids. Most small-molecule drugs are able to cross the stomach lining into the bloodstream where they travel throughout the body until they arrive at their therapeutic target.

Biologic drugs tend to be much larger than small-molecule drugs. Unlike small-molecule drugs, which are often synthetic chemicals which never occur naturally, many biologic drugs are synthetic versions of naturally-occurring proteins, such as growth factors, monoclonal antibodies, hormones, and immune-system signaling molecules. Most biologic drugs are larger and more complex than small-molecule drugs.

Small-molecule drugs differ from biologic drugs in the methods by which they are discovered and manufactured. As a result, these two types of drugs have markedly different therapeutic characteristics. These differences also have legal and regulatory consequences. For example, the types of patents used for small-molecule and biologic drugs, and the strategies for using (or attacking) these patents are also very different. Likewise, the regulatory and commercial considerations in gaining approval for new or follower small-molecule and biologic drugs are very different.

Figure 1 shows the structures of small-molecule and biologic versions of cancer drugs. Imatinib (sold in the U.S. as Gleevec and elsewhere as Glivec) is a small-molecule drug. Its chemical formula is relatively simple; it has fewer than 100 atoms and it works by inhibiting specific enzymes implicated in uncontrolled cell division. Pembrolizumab (sold as Keytruda) is much larger than imatinib. There are more than 20,000 atoms in pembrolizumab. It binds specific cell surface receptors and it works by blocking processes which inhibit cellular anti-tumor immune responses.

Small-molecule drugs such as imatinib tend to be available in orally-dosed forms (see Figure 2), but they can also frequently be dosed as patches or injections. Biologic drugs are generally unable to withstand stomach acids or to transit from the stomach into the bloodstream. They also tend to require constant refrigeration, so they may have much more limited dosage forms. Because of their special dosage

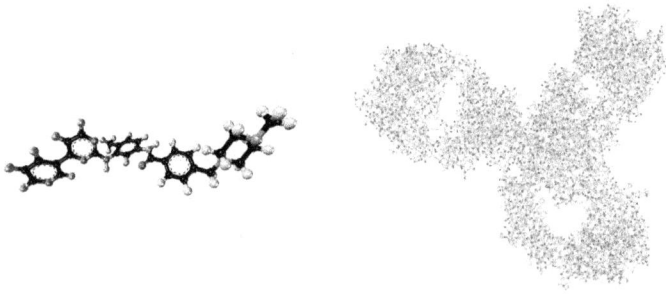

Figure 1: Imatinib (left) and pembrolizumab (right) chemical structures. Images are not to scale; pembrolizumab has roughly 200 times more atoms than imatinib. *Source: National Institutes of Health*

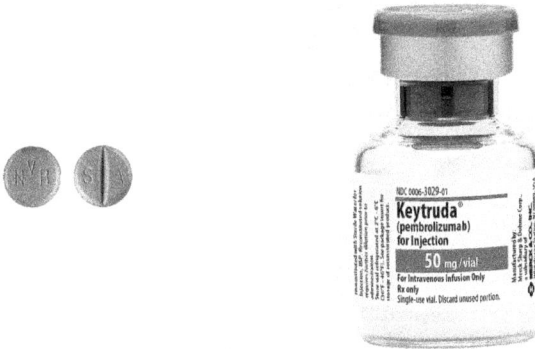

Figure 2: Gleevec (left) and Keytruda (right) dosage forms. *Sources: National Institutes of Health and company websites*

and storage requirements many biologic drugs are injected directly into patients in clinical settings. Administration in clinical settings, rather than via a pharmacist also has implications for drug marketing and uptake of follower drugs.

Many small-molecule drugs are chemically synthesized, which facilitates consistent mass-production for a relatively low cost. Biologics are made from living organisms. They may be sourced from human cell lines, from animals, or even microorganisms like yeast and bacteria. The more complex manufacturing processes for biologic drugs relative to small-molecule drugs tends to make production costs substantially higher.

BRANDED AND FOLLOWER DRUG APPROVAL

In the U.S. all drugs must be approved by the FDA. In the EU drug approvals are managed by the European Medicines Agency (EMA) or a member country's regulatory authority. Most other countries have single-country approval agencies, such as the National Medical Product Administration (NMDA; previously CFDA, and SFDA) in China, Health Canada, and the Pharmaceuticals and Medical Devices Agency (PMDA) in Japan.

The U.S. is the world's largest drug market, and its regulatory processes are similar to those in other countries, so for simplicity this section focuses on U.S. procedures.

The approval process for new innovative drugs and for follow-on drugs are very different. There are three basic mechanisms for small-molecule drugs. New small-molecule drugs are approved by submitting a New Drug Application (NDA) to the FDA. Generic drugs are approved through an Abbreviated New Drug Application (ANDA) process, and there is a hybrid process named by its regulatory section, 505(b)(2), which applies to modifications of new drugs which are neither novel, nor generics.

For biologics, new drugs and followers alike are approved by Biologics License Applications (BLAs). A way to differentiate between new new and biosimilar biologics is by the section of the Public Health Act under which they are approved. New biologic drugs are approved through section 351(a), and follower biosimilars are approved through section 351(k).

BRANDED DRUGS

While generic drugs and biosimilars can select development projects from the set of approved branded drugs, new drugs do not result from research and development efforts in a predictable way. It is not possible to project the cost or the likelihood of successful new drug development.

Imitation costs for drugs are much lower than the costs of initial research and development. So, once a drug is known to be safe and effective, it can generally be reverse-engineered without much difficulty. Without market protections for innovators, competitors would be able to produce copies of innovative drugs and sell them at a fraction of the cost of innovators, reflecting their greatly-reduced research and development costs.

The reason why patent protection and regulatory exclusivity are so important for branded drugs is that these market protections reward innovators for engaging in research areas with a high risk of failure. In the absence of protections companies, their employees, and their investors would lack the motivations to spend years and hundreds of millions of dollars researching and developing innovative new drugs.

The basic framework for new drug development is that once a drug candidate has been identified it is tested for indications of safety and efficacy in animal subjects. If these preclinical results are sufficiently promising the drug candidate is then tested in three phases of human clinical trials (see Figure 3), with costs increasing at each phase.

Phase I clinical trials involve a small number of healthy patients with a primary objective to simply establish safety and toxicity. If Phase 1 trials demonstrate sufficient safety then Phase 2 trials are initiated. These involve a larger number of participants for the purpose of establishing efficacy, in addition to safety. Phase 2 trials are also where dosage regiments are established. Phase 3 trials build on Phase 2 trials

Clinical Trials

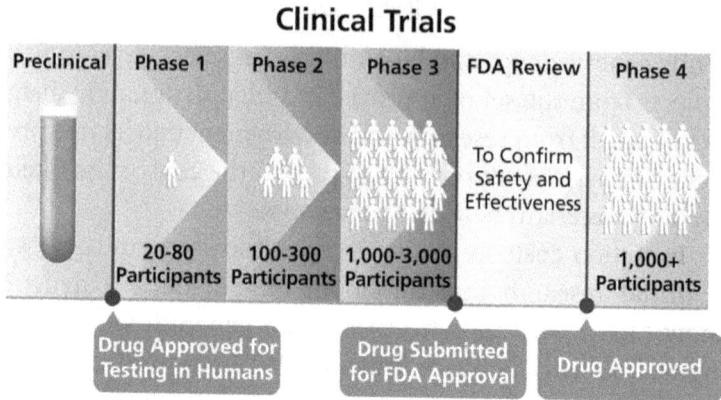

Preclinical	Phase 1	Phase 2	Phase 3	FDA Review	Phase 4
				To Confirm Safety and Effectiveness	
	20-80 Participants	100-300 Participants	1,000-3,000 Participants		1,000+ Participants

Drug Approved for Testing in Humans   Drug Submitted for FDA Approval   Drug Approved

Figure 3: Basic model of drug approval. *Source: National Institutes of Health*

to investigate efficacy in larger populations that better model the use of the drug should it be approved.

The length and cost of these trials varies by disease and also by the characteristics of each drug. Phase 4 trials follow approval to continue to monitor long-term effects of drugs once they are in the marketplace. These trials may be used to compare a new drug with alternatives to determine the relative therapeutic benefits and cost-effectiveness, and they may also aid in identifying additional uses for a drug.

The clinical trial process culminates in a drug application. In the U.S. the purpose of an NDA is to "tell the drug's whole story." This includes information on the ingredients of a drug, the results of preclinical tests, the outcomes of clinical trials, information on how a drug interacts with the body, and the drugs manufacturing, processing, packaging, and labelling. Essentially, the NDA contains all the information required to make an informed decision about the safety and efficacy of a proposed drug.

GENERIC DRUGS

According to the FDA, a generic drug is a copy of a branded drug that has the same dosage, safety, and strength.

The FDA review process is designed to ensure that generics perform the same way in the human body and have the same intended use as the branded medication. The purpose of this strict regulation is so that healthcare professionals and patients alike can substitute generic drugs for branded drugs without concern. The FDA uses multiple criteria to ensure that generic drugs perform comparably to branded drugs:

- The active ingredient in the generic medicine is the same as in the brand-name drug/innovator drug.
- The generic medicine has the same strength, use indications, form (such as a tablet or an injectable), and route of administration (such as oral or topical).
- The inactive ingredients of the generic medicine are acceptable.
- The generic medicine is manufactured under the same strict standards as the brand-name medicine.
- The container in which the medicine will be shipped and sold is appropriate, and the label is the same as the brand-name medicine's label.

One of the main facilitators of generic drug development in the U.S. is the Drug Price Competition and Patent Term Restoration Act, commonly referred to as the Hatch Waxman Act.

Before the act, generic drugs had to undergo the same lengthy and costly clinical testing as new drugs. Because of these burdens the number of generic drugs on the market was small. The Hatch-Waxman act enabled generic companies to cite safety and efficacy data from branded drug approvals. Generic entry was facilitated by enabling companies to gain generic approval by using the same active ingredient, dose, dosage form, and intended use as the original, and by demonstrating that their generic drugs were bioequivalent to an approved drug.

Prices Drop as More Generics Launch

An FDA analysis examined the impact of generic entry on drug prices and found that generic prices tend to drop only after two or more generic versions enter the market. They compared the average branded and generic prices for drugs to look for correlations between the number of generic manufacturers and the price of drugs.

They found that when there was just one generic entrant the generic drug prices tended to closely match branded prices (see Figure 4). A larger price difference was seen with a second generic entrant, and prices continued to decline with additional generic entrants.

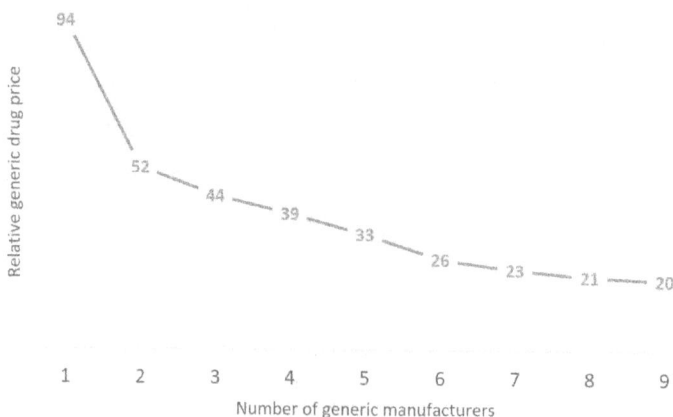

Figure 4: Generic competition reduces prices. *Source: FDA*

Generic Uptake Varies by Country

Numerous factors make generic drugs more or less attractive in different countries. The U.S., for example, is the world's largest drug market. It also features a lack of centralized price controls, which means that branded drugs can sell at higher prices than in other countries, and that generic entry is also simplified because generic manufacturers have more freedom in setting prices. These factors combine to make generic entry very attractive.

According to the OECD, development and adoption of generic drugs are universally viewed as opportunities to improve the efficiency of spending, but there are substantial differences in adoption (see Figure 5). They partially attribute the rates of generic adoption to differences in availability of generic medicines between countries, and they also acknowledge the important role played by policy decisions.

For example, prescribing by a drug's generic name (rather than its branded name) is permitted in many countries, and mandatory in others. The use of generic names on prescriptions aligns with substitution practices to drive generic usage. In many countries pharmacists are permitted to substitute branded drugs for generic equivalents; in some this

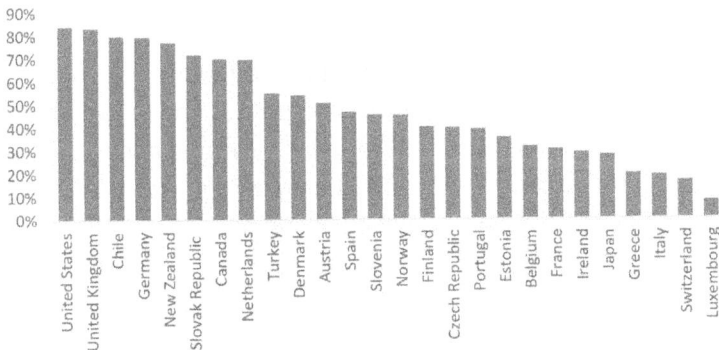

Figure 5: Generic adoption in various countries. *Source: OECD*

substitution is required.

Physician and pharmacist incentives also play a role. In France and Japan physicians have financial incentives to prescribe generic drugs. In some countries pharmacists are compensated through a mark-up on the price of medicine, which gives them a financial disincentive to dispense generics. Some countries have addressed this disincentive with policies to either match the branded-drug mark-up for generic prescriptions, or to provide direct incentives for generic substitutions.

The price of generic drugs is another area where policies differ between countries. In the U.S. generic manufacturers can set their own prices for drugs. By contrast, countries like New Zealand employ a tendering process to set generic drug prices. Another model used by some countries is to link generic prices to branded prices, setting an upper-limit for generics based on the price controls applied to the branded drugs.

When can Generics Launch?

Generic drugs can be marketed only after the relevant patents and regulatory exclusivities protecting the branded product expire. In many countries, including the U.S., *patent linkage* specifically prohibits generic approval before branded patents expire.

Patent linkage streamlines generic entry by linking patents with regulatory approval. This process creates an objective standard which benefits innovative and generic companies alike. For branded firms patent linkage provides them with an objective list of relevant patents to evaluate before filing for generic approval. Innovative firms benefit from patent linkage because it provides a simple method to prevent unauthorized generic launch prior to patent expiration.

Linkage can benefit branded and generic firms alike. By formalizing the generic approval process patent issues can be resolved before generic entry. Without patent linkage, branded firms would have to wait until generics launched and caused them *damages* and then they would need to sue generic companies to both stop generic sales and to recover their damages.

By linking patents to generic approval, generic companies can challenge branded patents without the risk of being found liable for damages, and branded firms do not have to wait until they have suffered damages to protect their patents. Importantly, patent linkage does not exist in the EU and in many other countries.

In the U.S. innovative drug companies are required to list patents protecting their drugs with the Food and Drug Administration (FDA). The FDA publishes these patents in a compendium called *Approved Drug Products with Therapeutic Equivalence Evaluations*, commonly known as the *Orange Book*. Drug developers must follow specific guidelines in listing their patents. Failure to list key patents, or listing of frivolous patents, may constitute patent misuse, which can lead to patent invalidation.

In seeking approval a generic manufacturer must file a certification to patents listed in the *Orange Book*. There are four basic options:

- A Paragraph I certification when the innovator has not filed patent information in the *Orange Book* (e.g. the drug was never patented).
- A Paragraph II certification when the *Orange Book*-listed patents are expired.
- A Paragraph III certification when the *Orange Book*-listed patents have not yet expired and the

generic company wishes to delay approval until patent expiration.

- A Paragraph IV certification when the *Orange Book*-listed patents are invalid or will not be infringed by generic entry.

For Paragraph I and Paragraph II certifications the FDA may grant an ANDA approval without delay. If an ANDA is filed with a Paragraph III or Paragraph IV certification the FDA may grant a *tentative* approval in anticipation of patent expiration and then grant a final approval on expiration of the relevant patent(s). For Paragraph IV there are complicated processes to handle patent challenge and invalidity claims. ANDA filers are required to notify the patentee of their ANDA filer with both a *notice letter* and *offer of confidential access* to the ANDA.

These documents must which meet specific requirements (a common branded company response is to challenge the legitimacy of these documents), and they must state the rationale behind these invalidity or non-infringement arguments. If the branded company responds to the notice letter within 45 days and files a patent infringement suit an automatic 30-month stay of ANDA marketing approval is placed on the drug. If patent expiration occurs within this 30 month period, if the 30-month period expires, or if a court determines the patent invalid within the 30 month period, the FDA can grant immediate approval to the ANDA. If the 30-month period expires before the patent issues have been resolved, then the generic firm may launch *at risk*, and they face damages should the patent infringement suit ultimately be decided in favor of the branded firm.

505(B)(2) HYBRID DRUG APPLICATIONS

Small-molecule drugs are commonly approved through one of three FDA regulatory pathways. These pathways are named by the subsections of the Food, Drug, and Cosmetics Act which describes them. The traditional NDA is described in section 505(b)(1); ANDAs for generic drugs is described in section 505(j), and; 505(b)(2) describes a hybrid between the NDAs and ANDAs.

Drugs approved by NDAs are typically called *branded* drugs, and ANDA-approved drugs are called *generic* drugs. Many names have been suggested for drugs approved under 505(b)(2), such as super generics, branded generics, value-added generics, and others. However, the best way to describe 505(b)(2) drugs is as a hybrid between a new and generic approval. Calling them super generics is inappropriate because in some cases a 505(b)(2) drug may be a substantial improvement over a branded drug (hence not really a generic), and it may even contain different ingredients than the reference drug.

The FDA outlines the important differences between the three modes. NDAs and 505(b)(2) applications must contain full reports on safety and efficacy, but only NDAs are required to have all studies conducted by, or for, the applicant. ANDAs and 505(b)(2) applications can include safety and efficacy reports not from the applicants, but ANDAs *cannot* contain safety or efficacy reports from the generic applicant — they can only cite those conducted by the NDA applicant.

505(b)(2) applications can amend or improve on prior NDAs. The applicant can cite prior studies demonstrating safety and efficacy of the elements already present in the reference listed drug. To demonstrate that the new elements (e.g. different dosage form, bioavailability, etc.) are safe and effective, *bridging* studies will need to demonstrate that the

Table: FDA regulatory frameworks for small-molecule drugs

New Drug NDA/(505)(b)(1)	Generic Drug ANDA/505(j)	Hybrid 505(b)(2)
Contains full reports of investigations of safety and effectiveness that were conducted by or for the applicant or for which the applicant has a right of reference or use.	Relies on FDA's finding that a previously approved reference listed drug is safe and effective … may not be submitted if clinical investigations are necessary to establish the safety and effectiveness of the proposed drug product.	Contains full reports of investigations of safety and effectiveness, where at least some of the information required for approval comes from studies not conducted by or for the applicant and for which the applicant has not obtained a right of reference or use.

Source: Food and Drug Administration

new attributes of the improved drug do not adversely affect safety or efficacy. There also exists an EU analog to the 505(b)(2) route, which is described in Article 10 (3) of EU DIRECTIVE 2001/83/ EC.

According to the FDA, the following changes may be included in 505(b)(2) applications:

- Changes in dosage form, strength, route of administration, formulation, dosing regimen
- New indications
- New combination product (e.g. substitution of an active ingredient in an approved combination product, or combining two independently-approved drugs)
- New active ingredient (e.g., different salt, ester complex, chelate, etc.)
- New molecular entity (e.g. prodrug or

metabolite of an approved drug)
- Rx/OTC switch (changing a prescription indication to an over-the-counter indication)

A recent research paper from Ingrid Freije, Stéphane Lamouche, and Mario Tanguay looked at hundreds of 505(b)(2) approvals to find out which types of changes were most common. As shown in Figure 6, new formulation or new manufacturer changes were most common, followed by new dosage forms and new combinations.

505(b)(2) drugs can bring increased convenience for patients, they can reduce side effects, and they can enhance the efficacy of drugs. Moreover, preferential dosage forms or reduced dosage frequencies can raise patient compliance rates. Because 505(b)(2) applications are filed as NDAs, they are eligible for all the same patent and regulatory exclusivities.

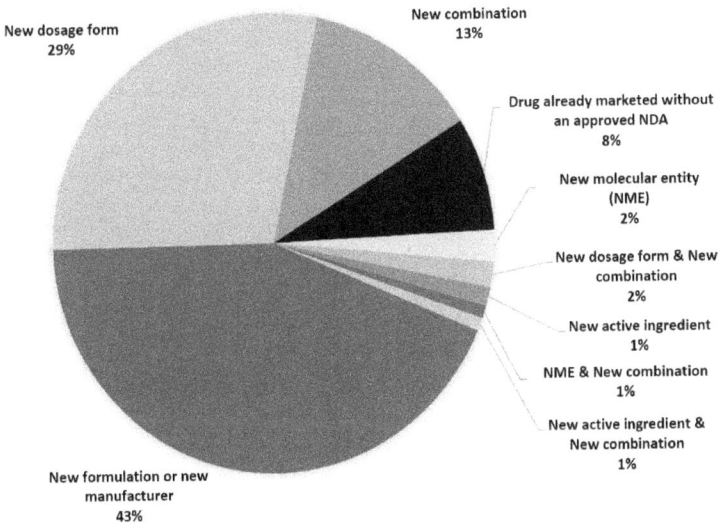

Figure 6: Approved 505(b)(2) changes. *Source: Freije, I., Lamouche, S., & Tanguay, M. (2019). Review of Drugs Approved via the 505(b)(2) Pathway: Uncovering Drug Development Trends and Regulatory Requirements. Therapeutic Innovation & Regulatory Science.*

For example, if a 505(b)(2) application includes a new chemical entity it may be eligible for 5-year regulatory exclusivity. If it includes new treatment indications it may receive 3-year regulatory exclusivity (seven years for an orphan indication). These topics are described in greater detail in the chapter on *Regulatory Exclusivity.*

Like ANDAs, 505(b)(2) applications cannot be granted if relevant patent or regulatory exclusivities exist. However, unlike ANDAs which are very limited in how much they can differ from branded drugs, 505(b)(2) applications can be used to gain approval for changes necessary to work around synthesis, method-of-use, or other patent claims. For example, Figure 7 shows Fresenius Kabi's 505(b)(2) approval for its intravenous powder version of Millenium's intravenous injectable drug Velcade (bortezomib).

DEPARTMENT OF HEALTH AND HUMAN SERVICES

Food and Drug Administration
Silver Spring MD 20993

NDA 205004

NDA APPROVAL

Fresenius Kabi USA, LLC
Attention: Arabella Buesching
Regulatory Specialist
Three Corporate Drive
Lake Zurich, IL 60047

Dear Ms. Buesching:

Please refer to your New Drug Application (NDA) dated November 30, 2012, received December 3, 2012, and your amendments, submitted pursuant to section 505(b)(2) of the Federal Food, Drug, and Cosmetic Act (FDCA) for Bortezomib for Injection, 3.5 mg/vial.

We acknowledge receipt of your amendment dated September 5, 2017, which constituted a complete response to our November 17, 2015, action letter.

This new drug application provides for the use of Bortezomib for Injection for the treatment of patients with multiple myeloma and for the treatment of patients with mantle cell lymphoma who have received at least 1 prior therapy.

We have completed our review of this application, as amended. It is approved, effective on the date of this letter, for use as recommended in the enclosed agreed-upon labeling text.

Figure 7: 505(b)(2) NDA approval for Fresenius Kabi improvements to bortezomib. *Source: FDA*

This case is also special because it included a first time reintroduction of the contents of a former version of the drug label. The original approval for Velcade was a second-line therapy for mantle cell lymphoma. Orphan drug exclusivity was granted specifically for "Treatment of patients with mantle cell lymphoma who have received at least 1 prior therapy." The label was later amended to include first-line treatment, so the indication was amended "to treatment of patients with mantle cell lymphoma," without a requirement for a prior therapy, with a new orphan drug exclusivity expiring in April 2022. Rather than wait for the orphan drug exclusivity to expire Fresenius Kabi successfully filed a 505(b)(2) application for the former label language — patients who had received at least 1 prior therapy.

505(b)(2) applications are hybrids by more than a regulatory definition. They also have commercial characteristics common to NDAs and generic drugs. For example, 505(b)(2) drugs do not require nearly as many studies as completely new drugs, so they are less expensive to develop and to approve. And, like generics, they also have much greater chances of being approved than completely new drugs. Accordingly, 505(b)(2) drugs can be profitably sold at lower prices than novel drugs, and they can obtain higher market shares and fetch higher prices than generic drugs.

BIOSIMILAR DRUGS

Since biologic drugs may be made from a variety of living sources, reproducing biologics is a more complex process than creating traditional generic drugs. For example, the maker of a biosimilar drug will almost certainly start with a different cell line than the original maker used. This may result in trivial, and in non-trivial, differences between the final biologic drug products which must be accounted for. Regulatory and patent issues for branded biologic and biosimilar drugs are therefore more complex than for small-molecule drugs.

According to FDA guidelines, biosimilars must be "highly-similar" to the reference branded drug. The biosimilar may have differences in "clinically inactive components" such as minor differences in the stabilizer or buffers in which the drug is stored, but there can be "no clinically meaningful differences."

A biosimilar application must include information supporting biosimilarity:

- Analytical studies demonstrating that the proposed biosimilar is highly similar to the reference product, notwithstanding minor differences in clinically inactive components
- Animal studies, including an assessment of toxicity
- Clinical studies demonstrating safety, purity, and potency of the proposed biosimilar product in one or more of the reference product indications

The case of Ortho Biotech's Eprex illustrates the challenges of maintaining consistency in biologic manufacturing. Eprex is a version of epoetin alfa, similar to Amgen's Epogen, which is marketed outside the U.S. The European Medicines Agency was concerned that Eprex was formulated with human serum albumin as a stabilizer. Out of fear that using purified human products in the formulation could facilitate the spread of diseases, the EMA asked for the drug be reformulated with a different stabilizer. Ortho responded by substituting Polysorbate 80 for human serum albumin.

After changing the formulation a small, but significant, increase in immunogenic responses emerged among patients taking Eprex. Ortho responded and launched a five-year, $100 million investigation. They ultimately discovered that the introduction of Polysorbate 80, a minor change in a non-therapeutic component of the drug, was causing problems in one of the many dosage forms of the drug. Polysorbate 80, which is an emulsifier often used in foods and cosmetics, was reacting with uncoated rubber stoppers used in pre-filled syringes where it was leaching allergenic compounds from the rubber stoppers.

This example of a simple alteration by the branded manufacturer causing unexpected problems highlights the challenges of biosimilar entry. Unlike generic small-molecules, where drug compounds can be demonstrated to be chemically identical and where there is strong historic evidence of which non-therapeutic formulation components can be substituted, biologics are harder to characterize and compare, and the impacts of changing formulations are also less certain.

An additional complication for biosimilars is proving interchangeability. Just because a biosimilar is approved does not mean that it can be substituted for the branded equivalent. According to the FDA, "an interchangeable product may be substituted for the reference product without the involvement of the prescriber." This standard means that with appropriate guidance on the interchangeability of drugs pharmacists should be free to substitute biosimilars for drugs without consulting the prescribing physician.

For interchangeability, the following conditions must be satisfied:

- The proposed interchangeable product should be expected to produce the same clinical result as the reference product in any given patient
- For a product administered more than once,

switching between the proposed interchangeable
product and the reference product does not
increase safety risks or decrease effectiveness
compared to using the reference product without
switching

Biologic drugs tend to cost more to manufacture than
small-molecule drugs, and the added burden of proving that
a biosimilar has no clinically meaningful differences further
increases the cost of developing and manufacturing a biosimilar relative to a generic small-molecule drug. Because of
these up-front and ongoing costs the savings for biosimilars
is less than for small-molecule generics. This is compounded
by the smaller number of biosimilar entrants relative to small-
molecule generics. While popular small-molecule drugs may
attract dozens of generic entrants, the reduced number of
biosimilar entrants and the complexity of interchangeability
will result in less competition for biologic drugs.

Biosimilar Naming

Unlike small-molecule drugs, where most generics are simply named by the drug's active ingredient, biosimilars use
proprietary names. This naming system reflects the reality
that biosimilars are likely to require more attention in substitution than small-molecule drugs. Also, not all biosimilars
will be interchangeable for branded drugs.

Accordingly, each biosimilar has a unique branded name
and they also have different ingredient names. For example,
the ingredient in Abbvie's Humira is adalimumab. The biosimilars are known as adalimumab-adaz, adalimumab-ad-
bm, and adalimumab-atto.

The rationale behind the suffixes is to distinguish biosimilars so that substitutions can be tracked and interchange-

Table: Biosimilar drug naming

Company	Ingredient Name	Branded Name
Abbvie	adalimumab	Humira
Sandoz	adalimumab-adaz	Hyrimoz
Boehringer Ingelheim	adalimumab-adbm	Cyltezo
Amgen	dalimumab-atto	Amjevita

ability can be more directed than small-molecule generics. Clearly, this complex naming scheme and the system for substitution can present a challenge for prescription of biosimilars, and its effect may be to strengthen the market for branded biologics.

Patents and Other Forms of Intellectual Property Protection

Intellectual property protection is essential for drug development. Unlike commodity-based industries, where competitive advantages may be gained through finding ways to produce goods for less money — through improved manufacturing processes, cheaper labor, or economies of scale in serving larger markets — drug development starts with innovation. For drugs, initial development costs can be punishingly high, while ongoing production costs are much lower. For example, the basic research process which identifies lead compounds for drugs is very expensive and many leads may advance to future stages only to fail after even further time and financial expenditures. Refinement and testing of lead compounds to produce a drug which is both safe and effective can ultimately take well over a decade and can cost hundreds of millions of dollars. But, the cost of manufacturing an approved drug can be relatively inexpensive. So, while the cost of innovation is high the cost of imitation is low.

Research and development must be financed by sales, which can only occur after research and development have been completed. Accordingly, innovation-based industries such as drug development rely on the ability to generate and exploit knowledge to gain a competitive advantage. And the ability to support post-innovation sales is conferred through intellectual property protection.

Intellectual property protection is necessary to secure a competitive advantage and it ultimately promotes innovation, as it enables innovators to prevent competitors from offering prices that reflect their vastly reduced research and development expenses. The temporary barrier to competition afforded by intellectual property protection permits innovators to sustain lengthy research efforts and to recoup their research and development costs.

Intellectual property differs from other forms of property (such as a parcel of land or a pair of shoes) because it is the product of intellectual effort and may be embodied as a concept rather than in a physical representation. There are four types of intellectual property rights: patent, trade secret, trademark, and copyright.

Patents allow an inventor to prevent others from practicing an invention without permission.

Trade secrets are unique among intellectual property rights in that they protect information and know-how that are not in the public domain.

Trademarks are words, symbols, or phrases used to identify a particular manufacturer or seller and their products and to distinguish them from others.

Copyrights protect the products of ideas — books, art, movies, etc. — but not the ideas themselves.

Patents, trade secrets and trademarks are described in greater detail below. Copyright has limited application for drug development, so it will not be discussed further.

PATENTS

Patents are of critical importance in drug development. The substantial financial costs, the long timelines to develop new drugs, and the high risk of failure motivate innovators to find ways to protect their markets. One of the key factors in deciding to proceed with a promising lead drug compound is the patentability of the drug. Likewise, for generic firms, lack of patent protection (or upcoming loss of exclusivity) is one of the primary factors in selecting which projects to pursue.

But, patents are not the only way to protect drugs. This chapter also discusses trade secrets and trademarks. The next chapter describes regulatory mechanisms used to balance market access and innovation.

A patent is a legal document that gives its owner the right to exclude others from making, using, selling, and importing an invention or the product of a patented process. The general term of a patent is 20 years from the date of filing, but there are many factors which can shorten or extend the life of a patent.

Patents provide protection only in the country or region in which they are granted. For example U.S. patent law grants the right to exclude others from making, using, offering for sale, or selling an invention in the U.S.

Independent patent applications must be filed for each country in which protection is desired, although regional patent offices such as the African Intellectual Property Organization, the African Regional Intellectual Property Organization, the Eurasian Patent Organization, the European Patent Organisation, and the Patent Office of the Cooperation Council for the Arab States of the Gulf enable patent protection in multiple countries.

The commentary in this section is specific to the U.S. patent system, with important differences in other countries highlighted as necessary.

WHAT CAN BE PATENTED?

To understand patents it is useful to ask why governments grant patents. The basic motivations for granting patents are that a) offering patents drives innovation by providing a temporary monopoly period in which innovators can recoup their time and financial expenditures, and b) requiring innovators to disclose the processes essential to their inventions can liberate knowledge which would otherwise never be disclosed. The opportunity to examine the methods to practice an invention can help develop non-infringing alternatives and improvements, and it can also hasten the entry of competitors after patents expire.

The scope of innovation tends to mirror the scope of patent protection. For many innovative firms the first question in evaluating whether to invest in a promising drug lead is how protectable the market for the drug would be. Without patent protection it is difficult to justify the risk and expense of drug development.

In the U.S. patents are available for one of four principle categories of inventions:

- a composition of matter
- a process
- a machine
- an article of manufacture

These categories are described in Section 101 of the patent code, so failure to satisfy this requirement is often called a Section 101 invalidation.

Beyond meeting the Section 101 requirements, patentable inventions must also be novel, useful, and non-obvious. Section 102 describes novelty, and Section 103 describes non-obviousness, so invalidations based on these factors tends to likewise be named after the relevant patent code sections. These additional criteria are very important, and they are common targets for invalidation arguments.

The novelty of an invention is critical. In most countries it is not possible to patent an invention after it has been publicly disclosed. The mere mention of an invention at a conference or in a research publication can render it unpatentable. In the U.S. disclosures by an inventor may be permitted one year or less prior to patent filing. Because most drugs are likely to be sold internationally it is generally preferred to ensure that no disclosure occurs prior to patent filing.

To be patentable an invention must be useful. In response to unrealistic utility being claimed in patents (e.g. claiming that a complex and expensive drug compound could be used as landfill, rather than revealing its therapeutic benefits) the utility must be "specific and substantial." According to the USPTO guidelines, the invention should "provide a well-defined and particular benefit to the public" in a "real world" context.

Just as the definition of what is *novel* changes over time, so does the threshold for obviousness. What is not obvious at one time may later be deemed obvious. For example, adding a chemical group to a drug may unexpectedly change its characteristics. Subsequently adding that same chemical group to similar drugs may be deemed obvious if the elicited change becomes predictable. Importantly, the threshold for *obviousness* is based on an analysis of whether the invention would have been obvious to a hypothetical "person of ordinary skill in the art" at the time of patent filing. Just as prior disclosures of an invention can result in a Section 102 invalidation, statements regarding the obviousness of an invention (such as company materials claiming that their techniques can predictably and reliably improve drugs) may be used to invalidate key patents.

WHEN DO DRUG PATENTS EXPIRE?

Calculating drug patent expiration dates can be an involved process. The general rule for patents filed after 1995 is that the patent expires 20 years from the date of filing. Because there are special patent extensions available for drugs, the answer is almost always more complicated. Also, not all patents block generic approval, so simply looking at the first- or last-expiring patent is not an effective way to determine when generic drugs can enter the market.

Patent Term Extension

A unique aspect of drugs, relative to most other products, is that drugs cannot be marketed until they are proven safe and effective. The Hatch-Waxman Act allows patent owners to recover time spent in clinical trials and waiting for FDA regulatory review.

Because patents must be filed prior to clinical trials, valuable market exclusivity can be lost. This means that without the Hatch-Waxman patent extensions, drugs would have shorter effective patent-protected periods than other inventions. To soften the burden of researching innovative drugs which might require extensive clinical trials and possibly protracted FDA review, an extra half-day restoration of patent life is available for every day of clinical trials and day-for-day restoration is available for the FDA review period.

There are two restrictions on restoration: The effective life of a drug patent cannot exceed 14 years, and the total time restored cannot exceed five years.

There are some important strategic considerations to employing Hatch-Waxman extensions. A patent's term can be extended only once, only one patent can be extended for a given regulatory review period, and extensions are limited to the first approved use of a drug.

So, if a single patent protects multiple drugs, the Hatch-Waxman extensions can only apply to the review time of one of the drugs. Further, if multiple patents protect a single drug, only one of those patents can be extended. Also, only the first approved use of a drug is eligible for patent term extension. For a drug in development which has applications for multiple diseases, careful consideration of the timelines of development and the likelihood of FDA approval for each indication may need to be balanced against the revenue expectations so that patent extensions can be directed for the greatest benefit.

Several tools are available to simplify determining (or at least estimating) patent expiration dates. Firstly, in the U.S. the FDA requires companies to list relevant patents protecting their drugs, along with the expiration dates. These drug-patent linkages are published in the publication *Approved Drug Products with Therapeutic Equivalence Evaluations*, commonly known as the *Orange Book*. While one must still analyze these patents to assess which are likely to block generic approval, the inclusion of objective expiration dates greatly facilitates planning.

The FDA acts as a "custodian" of the *Orange Book*, listing and amending patent data according to company requests. While the FDA has not historically policed errors and omissions in *Orange Book* listings, it is vital that companies accurately follow FDA guidelines. According the the FDA, NDA applicants *must* list drug substance (active ingredient) patents, drug product (formulation and composition) patents, and method-of-use patents. NDA applicants *may not* list process patents, patents claiming packaging, patents claiming metabolites, and patents claiming intermediates.

Listing patents outside the required scope, failure to list required patents, or misstating expiration dates may be construed as patent misuse, and the penalty for patent misuse can be punitive — it may result in invalidation of a patent.

For U.S. patents not in the *Orange Book*, the Patent and Trademark Office (USPTO) has a patent term calculator available at https://www.uspto.gov/patent/laws-and-regulations/patent-term-calculator.

Outside the U.S. the simplest starting point is to estimate the earliest possible expiration date as 20 years from the filing date of the first patent in a family (patents filed in multiple countries may be arranged into *families*). Country-specific patent extensions can then be considered and the actual loss-of-exclusivity date can be confirmed with local counsel.

It is also important to consider the potential for earlier-than-anticipated expirations. For example, patent owners must make regular maintenance payments over the life of a patent. Not making the necessary maintenance payments — by intent or by mistake — can result in premature expiration. Patent challenges may also invalidate patents. A common tactic for generic firms is to invalidate patents so they can be the first to offer a lower-cost version of branded drugs. Even if patents are not invalidated their claims can be amended during the life of a patent, which can open the opportunity for generic entry years earlier than expected.

Alternatively, six months of pediatric exclusivity can be added to patents (see the next chapter), extending their expiration dates. While the claimed elements of a patent become public domain on expiration, innovators may file follow-on patents as key patent expirations loom. These follow-on patents may cover important inventions, such as cost-effective manufacturing techniques or improvements to the drug which can alter vital aspects of generic entry (see more in the chapter on *Branded Drugs*).

Supplementary Protection Certificates

Market exclusivity in the EU can be extended through supplementary protection certificates (SPCs). Similar to patent extensions in the U.S., in the EU SPCs are designed to help innovators recover patent protection lost due to the time period between filing patents and obtaining regulatory marketing approval. SPCs extend the effective protection of products already on the market by a maximum of 5 years following patent expiry. There is also a 15-year cap on the overall duration of patent and SPC.

THE "RIGHT TO EXCLUDE"

An important factor in patent law is that patents confer only the right to exclude. They do not grant the right to practice an invention. This is important in the context of drugs, because the marketing and distribution of drugs is controlled by separate regulatory authorities from those which grant patents. In the U.S. the USPTO grants patents, while the FDA regulates the marketing and distribution of drugs. FDA approval is necessary to sell a drug; patents can only be used to stop others from selling drugs.

For example, after the U.S. Department of Health and Human Services obtained patent 6,630,507 covering "Cannabinoids as Antioxidants and Neuroprotectants" many proponents for federal legalization of cannabis excitedly cited the government's patent as an indication of a softening of the government's stance on cannibis and predicted de-scheduling by the Drug Enforcement Administration. However, patent grants by the USPTO are not indicative of whether or not it is legal to use inventions. Despite the mention of medical uses in the patent's title and claims, the patent has no bearing on the Drug Enforcement Administration's inclusion of cannabis on *Schedule I* ("drugs with no currently accepted medical use and a high potential for abuse") or on FDA determinations of its safety and efficacy.

LICENSING AND SELLING PATENTS

As a form of *intellectual* property, patents can be exchanged, sold, and rented, similar to physical property. Because of stratification in drug development and commercialization, there are companies which specialize in inventing lead compounds for drugs, in developing drugs from lead compounds, and in manufacturing and selling approved drugs. It is common for drug companies specializing in the latter segments to secure licenses conveying rights to use patents, or to purchase patents outright from the inventing firms.

Patent licenses can also enable firms to divide and share markets. For example it is common for companies without strong multinational presences to retain rights in their home country and to license territorial rights in other countries to domestic or multinational partners. Alternatively companies may retain rights to select disease categories and license other uses.

Innovative firms can even license "authorized generic" versions of their branded drugs enabling them to earn revenues in both branded and generic markets (for more see *Authorized Generics* in the chapter on *Branded Drugs*).

TRADE SECRETS

Unlike patents, which provide time-limited monopoly periods in exchange for disclosure of how to practice inventions, trade secrets offer the potential for unlimited protection and they do not require disclosure. A downside of trade secrets relative to patents is that they can be lost through reverse-engineering, independent invention, or poor control of information.

A disadvantage of trade secrets, when compared to patents, is that they do not grant the right to exclude others from practicing an invention. If a competitor is able to independently develop or reverse-engineer an invention, or if the owner of the secret accidentally makes it public, then there is little recourse for preventing use. Courts may refuse to recognize a trade secret if reasonable efforts have not been made to keep the information from being disclosed.

In the book *Making PCR* it is explained that the inventor of the polymerase chain reaction (PCR), a vital technique for forensics and for research, had considered using trade secret protection to prevent competitors from using the key enzyme essential for the process. Because of the perceived ease of using reverse-engineering to identify the key enzyme for PCR it was decided that patenting conferred better protection. Similarly, if a competitor is able to independently discover the same method as protected by a trade secret, then the original inventor has no means to prevent them from employing it.

Finally, trade secrets must be kept secret. Unlike patents, where the means to practice an invention are published, accidental disclosure of a trade secret can leave an inventor unable to control its use.

Accordingly, trade secrets may be very effective in protecting manufacturing processes, which are generally performed out of public view. These processes may be essential to reducing the cost of manufacture or to ensuring quality and consistency of production, so keeping them as trade secrets can be an effective way to exclude competitors. By contrast the key compounds vital for a drug's activity are generally available for examination and reverse-engineering by competitors once they are sold to the public, which makes patenting a preferable option.

Trade secrets are also useful for processes which are not subject to reverse engineering, such as in-house manufacturing, drug screening and related techniques, and compiled computer programs, where control of the protected invention is maintained by the owner. Processes which cannot be patented, perhaps because of little-known prior art, are also good candidates for trade secret protection.

Processes for which patents would be difficult to enforce, such as drug screening or other methods which cannot be publicly observed or for which it would be difficult to prove infringement may also be best protected as trade secrets.

A significant disadvantage of patents, relative to trade secrets, is that patents eventually expire and require disclosure of the best mode to practice an invention, which may necessitate the publication of trade secrets involved in production processes. Furthermore, because it is not possible to anticipate all the possible applications of an invention, patent publication may inadvertently facilitate the development of non-infringing competing products. In deciding how best to protect an invention these significant differences necessitate weighing the near-term protective effects of patents against the long-term benefits of trade secrets.

The example of Premarin illustrates the effective use of trade secret protection, as well as the tactics essential to limiting access to those secrets and excluding violators.

Premarin is an estrogen hormone therapy developed by Wyeth. The drug is produced from the urine of pregnant mares through a complex purification process (hence the name, PREgnant MARe urINe).

Wyeth filed patents for several methods connected with manufacturing Premarin, but they decided to maintain a key procedure, known as the Brandon process (the drug is produced in Brandon in the Canadian province of Manitoba), as a trade secret. They employed several precautions to protect the Brandon process. Employees were required to sign confidentiality agreements, and the Brandon process was not even committed to paper until the FDA demanded it.

Premarin was first sold by Wyeth in 1942, and the last of its patents expired in 1975. But because the production processes remained secret there was no way for generics to enter the market efficiently. Sales peaked at $2 billion in 2002, and ultimately dropped following a National Institutes of Health-sponsored study that showed negative outcomes from long-term use of estrogen hormone replacement therapy.

During its productive selling years many potential generic entrants sought approval for synthetically-produced versions of the drug. Wyeth was able to repeatedly convince the FDA that differences between Premarin and the synthetically-derived alternatives required a full, non-generic, drug application. This changed when Natural Biologics set out to produce a generic Premarin from horse urine in an attempt to avoid the equivalence issues which plagued the synthetic versions. Wyeth responded by suing Natural Biologics for trade secret theft, before any generic drug could be sold.

The discovery of extensive communications between Natural Biologics' CEO and a former Wyeth scientist, which coincided with improvements in Natural Biologics' generic Premarin program, made a strong case for trade secret theft, ultimately helping Wyeth win the lawsuit. Unlike a patent infringement suit, where a pre-launch generic challenger may simply be denied FDA approval, the punishment doled for Natural Biologics was punitive. The company was ordered to destroy all research materials and drug supplies, and its leaders were forever barred from the estrogen replacement market.

TRADEMARK

A trademark is a word, symbol, or phrase used to identify a particular manufacturer or seller and their products, and to distinguish them from others.

Unlike patents, trademark rights can last indefinitely if the owner continually uses the mark to identify its goods or services. Trademarks can also extend to the look and feel of a product or logo, provided it does not confer any sort of functional or competitive advantage. Drug companies often trademark both the names and the physical characteristics of their drugs, which is why generic drugs have different names and look different from branded products.

Using trademark protection to sustain branded drug sales post-patent expiration generally works best for drugs which are used repeatedly over a long timeframe, and those which are purchased directly by patients (as opposed to requiring a prescription). For example, most common over-the-counter painkillers such as Tylenol and Advil are placed on store shelves alongside their generic counterparts. Persistent marketing efforts maintain consumer familiarity with the trade names, influencing purchase preferences.

Trademark protection can extend beyond the names of drugs into the "look and feel" of products as well. In a prominent example, Nexium was successfully branded as the *purple pill* (see Figure 1). In fact, the consumer information website for Nexium is at www.purplepill.com. To strengthen the brand association AstraZeneca also trademarked the pill color. As stated on Nexium's website, "NEXIUM and the color purple as applied to the capsule are registered trademarks of the AstraZeneca group of companies."

The rights to a trademark can be lost through abandonment, improper licensing, or genericity. Historically, non-use of a trademark for three consecutive years has been considered evidence of abandonment. Maintaining adherence in

Figure 1: Nexium from AstraZeneca (purple pills), left, and generic esomeprazole from Teva (teal pills), right. *Source: National Institutes of Health*

licensing is important as well.

One reason why many companies have very specific guidelines regarding the representation of their trademarks is that a trademark licensed without adequate control by the owner may become unenforceable. If a trademark no longer positively identifies the goods of a particular provider then it becomes challenging to argue that it distinguishes one product from another.

Trademarks that are originally unique can also become generic over time. A trademark is considered generic when, in the minds of a substantial majority of the public, the word denotes a type of product and not a specific source or manufacturer. A relevant example of the loss of a trademark to genericity is Bayer's loss of its Aspirin trademark. Because the word aspirin was consistently used without the product descriptor *pain reliever* following it, aspirin became a generic term for pain reliever and was therefore no longer protected under trademark law. Today Bayer's aspirin is sold under the tradename *Bayer® extra strength aspirin for migraine pain* alongside generic aspirin.

For more details on the different types of names used to identify drugs see the appendix on *Drug Names*

Regulatory Exclusivity

In addition to protections derived from patents, the FDA and other regulators may grant market exclusivity to drugs meeting specific conditions. The motivation to grant exclusivity is to foster innovation and to promote the development of drugs for applications that might otherwise offer insufficient motivation.

Patents and regulatory exclusivity work in a similar fashion but are distinct from one another and governed by different statutes. Patents are a property right granted by the U.S. Patent and Trademark Office. They may be enforced at any time and can encompass a wide range of claims. Regulatory exclusivity is granted by the U.S. Food and Drug Administration and similar regulatory bodies in other countries, and prevents the regulatory approval of competitor drugs.

While some regulatory exclusivities such as pediatric clinical trial exclusivity are attached to the end of patents, in most cases patents and regulatory exclusivity are independent. For example, patents can be asserted against drugs which are in development, against drugs for which approval is sought, or after a drug launches. By contrast, regulatory exclusivity tends to affect only drug approvals.

SMALL-MOLECULE DRUGS

NEW CHEMICAL ENTITY

New Chemical Entity exclusivity (NCE), also known as new drug product exclusivity, grants a five-year period of exclusivity. During this period the FDA cannot approve a drug application containing the same drug, so even if competitors find new indications for a compound with NCE exclusivity they cannot enter the market. Also, the FDA will not even review a generic application until one year before the exclusivity expires. This is where the term NCE-1 comes from, as many generics may rush to file patent challenges on the NCE-1 date in the hope of being the first to win 180-day generic exclusivity (see *Patent Challenge*, below).

The NCE-1 date is generally four years from a drug's approval date but in the case of an extension for pediatric clinical trials (see below), the effective exclusivity period is 5.5 years. Accordingly, the earliest date for ANDA submission in these cases is 4.5 years after approval.

NEW CLINICAL INVESTIGATION

If a drug application requires new clinical investigations, it may be eligible for a three-year New Clinical Investigation (NCI) exclusivity. This period of exclusivity is frequently applied to new formulations of drugs, to new dosage forms, and to drugs after an "Rx-to-OTC switch."

Importantly, NCI exclusivity only applies to the new form of the drug. As loss-of-exclusivity dates for branded drugs loom, companies frequently develop more attractive options to extend the brand. For example, a brand may be able to obtain NCI protection for extended-release formulations which enable patients to take fewer pills per day. This can differentiate the extended-release version of branded drug from generic entrants, which would only be able to sell the original version of the the drug. Likewise, demonstrating that a drug is safe enough to be sold over the counter, rather than by prescription can increase branded market share even after generics launch.

NCI exclusivity may prevent generics from selling a new drug form, but the brand extension may still depend on patient and payer preferences. For example, most payers require drugs to demonstrate better patient outcomes than existing alternatives. If reformulating a drug from two pills per day to one daily pill does not produce measurable clinical improvements then payers may require patients to pay out-of-pocket for the new version.

PEDIATRIC CLINICAL TRIALS EXCLUSIVITY

The term of most forms of exclusivity is based on the approval date of the drug. Pediatric exclusivity is different. It adds 6 months to existing patent protection or regulatory exclusivity.

The motivation for regulators to grant pediatric exclusivity is that many drugs are never tested in pediatric populations, leaving physicians ill-equipped to make informed prescription decisions. Companies that complete FDA-requested pediatric clinical investigations (it is possible to ask the FDA to request these trials) can be granted two separate six month extensions. Importantly, companies do not need to gain, or even file for, pediatric indications to receive the extensions; they need only perform the requested studies.

Pediatric exclusivity is usually granted shortly before a patent expires, so it is important to consider the opportunity for a patent to receive this extension in timing generic entry.

ORPHAN DRUG

Rare diseases present a special case for drug companies and policymakers. Because of the relative lack of familiarity among physicians, patients may need see many specialists before they can be properly diagnosed (if at all). Further, patients may need to travel great distances to receive treatments. The extra burdens faced by patients with rare diseases is compounded by the lack of motivation which innovative firms may have for developing treatments for small populations. Accordingly, orphan drug exclusivity creates special incentives for encourage companies to develop drugs for rare diseases.

In the U.S. the Orphan Drug Act provides incentives for companies that develop treatments for conditions affecting fewer than 200,000 Americans, or those that affect more than 200,000 Americans for which there is no reasonable expectation that the cost of research and development will be recovered from U.S. sales.

Companies that successfully develop an orphan drug in the U.S. are given clinical testing grants, tax credits for the costs of clinical trials, and seven years of market exclusivity for approved products, regardless of patent protection. Similar programs exist in other countries as well.

In the EU, orphan drug status is granted to drugs for the treatment, prevention or diagnosis of a disease that is life-threatening or chronically debilitating, for which there is no satisfactory alternative, and for which the prevalence in the EU is not be more than 5 in 10,000 (similar to the U.S. prevalence) or it must be unlikely that marketing of the medicine would generate sufficient returns to justify the investment needed for its development. Eligible drugs can benefit from 10 years of market exclusivity, an accelerated approval process, and fee reductions.

PATENT CHALLENGE

A key provision of the Hatch-Waxman Act is that ANDA filers with Paragraph IV certifications who successfully invalidate a patent can obtain 180 days of marketing exclusivity. Originally this exclusivity was available to the first eligible filer.

Following problems with generic filers lining up days in advance or requesting security camera footage to secure first-filer status, all first-day filers with eligible ANDAs can share the 180-day exclusivity regardless of the exact time of submission.

If any of the first-day filers can successfully invalidate a key patent, then all companies with Paragraph IV-containing ANDAs filed on the same date may share the same 180-day exclusivity period.

GENERATING ANTIBIOTIC INCENTIVES NOW

The *Generating Antibiotic Incentives Now* (GAIN) Act encourages the development of new antibiotics.

Under the GAIN Act, sponsors may request a Qualified Infectious Disease Product (QIDP) designation. GAIN makes qualified drugs eligible for an additional five years of marketing exclusivity.

This means that new chemical entities may benefit from 10 years of market exclusivity and orphan drugs may benefit from 12 years of marketing exclusivity. Qualified drugs are also eligible for fast track designation and priority review.

COMPETITIVE GENERIC THERAPY

The FDA established the Competitive Generic Therapies (CGTs) pathway to encourage generic entry for drugs that face inadequate competition. This framework provides incentives for developing generic versions of drugs that currently face little or no competition.

Designation of a drug as a CGT can be granted when is only one approved drug, or if there are no approved drugs listed in the *Orange Book* (see *Finding Low-Competition Opportunities* in the chapter on *Generic Entry* for more information). Under the CGT pathway the FDA may expedite its review and the first-approved CGT drug application may be eligible for 180 days of marketing exclusivity.

BIOLOGIC DRUGS

The regulatory framework for biologic drugs is very different from the framework for small-molecules. As described in *Small-Molecule and Biologic Drugs* in the chapter on *Innovative and Follower Drugs*, biologic drugs tend to be much larger than small-molecule drugs and they are much more complex to manufacture, to compare, and to formulate into dosage forms.

The regulatory pathway and the incentives for new and follower biologics are still evolving. Follower biologic drugs may be approved under an expedited biosimilar approval pathway which is more complex than the ANDA process for small-molecule drugs.

The basic criteria for biosimilar entry is that the follower biologic have "no clinically meaningful differences" from the branded biologic. If a biosimilar can be demonstrated to be safe and effective enough for pharmacists to substitute for branded drugs without any interaction from the prescribing physician then it can be designated as "interchangeable."

Similar to the four-year NCE-1 period during which the FDA cannot receive an ANDA for a new chemical entity, for biologics the FDA cannot receive a biosimilar application until four years after the original BLA date. Further, the FDA cannot approve a biosimilar until 12 years after the original BLA. Biologics are also eligible for six-month pediatric exclusivity and seven-year orphan drug exclusivity. The first company to develop an interchangeable biosimilar can obtain up to one year of market exclusivity from other biosimilars.

Analyzing Patents and Litigation

PATENTS AS SOURCES OF INFORMATION

While the primary purpose of patents are as legal instruments to confer rights and privileges on their owners, they may also contain valuable technical information about inventions which is not published elsewhere.

Patents also contain contact information about the inventors. Knowing who played a key role in inventing a drug can be commercially useful. For example, key inventors may be tapped as consultants or advisors on projects which do not conflict with their non-compete agreements.

PATENT CLAIMS

There are many excellent guides available describing how to read patents. Many of these guides are very technical, which is warranted because patents are highly structured documents and virtually all the parts of a patent are legally significant. This section presents a very brief overview of a patent with the goal of helping you extract useful information (hint:

read the claims).

The basic components of a patent are the cover page and the specification. The cover page contains predominantly bibliographic information about a patent (see Figure 1). It lists the title, inventors, the assignee (or patent owner), important dates, technology categories, and other elements. These elements are important for legal and regulatory reasons. They can also be used to extract technical information. For example, by identifying the inventors it is possible to look at their research publications and other patents to expand on the technical descriptions included in the patents. The title and abstract may serve as useful summaries of the scope of the patent, but a much better place to look is the claims, described below.

Figure 2 shows the summary for patent 4,659,716, which protects Claritin. The title and abstract provide clues of the

---

United States Patent [19]

Villani et al.

[11] **Patent Number:** 4,659,716

[45] **Date of Patent:** Apr. 21, 1987

[54] ANTIHISTAMINIC 8-(HALO)-SUBSTITUTED 6,11-DIHYDRO-11-(4-PIPERIDYLIDENE)-5H-BENZO[5,6]CYCLOHEPTA[1,2-b]PYRIDINES

[75] Inventors: Frank J. Villani, Fairfield; Jesse K. Wong, Union, both of N.J.

[73] Assignee: Schering Corporation, Madison, N.J.

[21] Appl. No.: 838,974

[22] Filed: Mar. 12, 1986

Related U.S. Application Data

[63] Continuation-in-part of Ser. No. 580,304, Feb. 15, 1984, abandoned.

[51] Int. Cl.⁴ A61K 31/445; C07D 401/08
[52] U.S. Cl. 514/290; 546/93
[58] Field of Search 546/93; 514/290

[56]   **References Cited**

U.S. PATENT DOCUMENTS

3,326,924 6/1967 Villani 546/93
3,717,647 2/1973 Villani 546/315
4,282,233 8/1981 Villani .... 546/93 X

FOREIGN PATENT DOCUMENTS

46-20387 6/1971 Japan 546/93

OTHER PUBLICATIONS

PDR, 1984, pp. 515, 529, 557, 558, 566, 593, 594, 611, 631, 633, 648, 664, 667, 668, 709.
Scrip No. 1026, 8/19/85.
Burger's Medicinal Chemistry, 4th Ed, Part III, Wiley–Interscience, NY, 1981, pp. 818–819.
Brandon, M., et al., Annals of Allergy, 44, 71–75 (1980).
Business Week, 5/2/83, pp. 60–61.
Villani, F., et al., Arzneim.–Forsch., 36(11), Nr. 9 1986, pp. 1311–1314.
Villani, F. et al., J. Med. Chem., 15(7), 750–754 (1972).
Goodman and Gilman's, The Pharmacological Basis of Therapeutics, MacMillan, New York, 1980, p. 626.
PDR, 1985, pp. 888, 889, 964, 1425, 1426, 1485, 1612, 1613, 1725, 1726, 1872, 1873, 1879, 1965, 1966, 2276, 2277.

Primary Examiner—Richard A. Schwartz
Attorney, Agent, or Firm—James R. Nelson; Stephen I. Miller; Richard C. Billups

[57]   **ABSTRACT**

Disclosed are 7- and/or 8-(halo or trifluoromethyl)-substituted-6,11-dihydro-11-(4-piperidylidene)-5H-benzo[5,6]cyclohepta[1,2-b]pyridines and the pharmaceutically acceptable salts thereof, which possess antihistaminic properties with substantially no sedative properties. Methods for preparing and using the compounds and salts are described.

16 Claims, No Drawings

Figure 1: Cover page for patent 4,659,716. Source: USPTO

Summary for Patent: 4,659,716

Title:	Antihistaminic 8-(halo)-substituted 6,11-dihydro-11-(4-piperidylidene)-5H-benzo[5,6]cyclohepta[1,2-b]pyridin es
Abstract:	Disclosed are 7- and/or 8-(halo or trifluoromethyl)-substituted-6,11-dihydro-11-(4-pipendylidene)-5H-benzo[5,6]cyclohepta[1,2-b]pyridines and the pharmaceutically acceptable salts thereof, which possess antihistaminic properties with substantially no sedative properties. Methods for preparing and using the compounds and salts are described.
Inventor(s):	Villani, Frank J (Fairfield, NJ), Wong, Jesse K. (Union, NJ)
Assignee:	Schering Corporation (Madison, NJ)
Application Number:	06/838,974
Patent Litigation and PTAB cases:	See patent lawsuits and PTAB cases for patent 4,659,716
Patent Claim Types: see list of patent claims	Compound; Composition; Dosage form; Use;

Figure 2: Summary of patent 4,659,716. *Source: DrugPatentWatch*

patent's scope. A suggested profile of the claim types is also provided, but it is only by examining the claims that the scope of the patent can be precisely determined.

Beyond the cover page are various background descriptive sections, followed by the claims. According to the USP-TO:

> The specification must include a written description of the invention and of the manner and process of making and using it, and is required to be in such full, clear, concise, and exact terms as to enable any person skilled in the technological area to which the invention pertains, or with which it is most nearly connected, to make and use the same.
>
> The specification must set forth the precise invention for which a patent is solicited, in such manner as to distinguish it from other inventions and from what is old. It must describe

completely a specific embodiment of
the process, machine, manufacture,
composition of matter, or improvement invented, and must explain
the mode of operation or principle
whenever applicable. The best mode
contemplated by the inventor for car-
rying out the invention must be set
forth.

The specification includes the title and abstract of the invention, a background of the invention, a brief summary of
the invention, a detailed description of the invention, at least
one claim, and it may include drawings.

The purpose of the claims is to precisely define the scope
of the invention that the patent protects. Examination of the
claims is vital to understanding the scope of the patent and
how it applies to blocking infringing novel or generic drugs.
Much thought and careful planning can go into developing
patent claims, and their interpretation can be the focus of
pivotal court decisions.

The other sections of the specification support the patentability of the claims. As explained by the USPTO, "the
claims must find clear support or antecedent basis in the
description." These sections should explain why a patent is
not obvious. To support the non-obviousness of an invention
specification may also mention failed efforts which preceded
the invention. Finally, the specification should make a clear
and compelling case for the utility of the claimed matter.

In providing the basis for the patent claims, the background and description sections provide extensive background information related to the invention. If previously
protected trade secrets (see *Trade Secrets*, in the chapter on
Patents and Other Forms of Intellectual Property) need to be

exposed to support the claims, then their publication in the patent may result in loss of trade secret protection. The sections supporting the claims can be very useful in finding opportunities to invalidate a patent. They can also help identify related science that can provide opportunities for other patents, or they can make the case that certain research paths are unlikely to be successful and should be abandoned. Once a patent expires, the information contained in these sections can also help others learn how to practice the invention.

Figure 3 shows the full set of sixteen claims in patent

We claim:

1. A compound of the formula

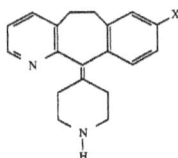

or a pharmaceutically acceptable salt thereof, wherein X represents Cl or F.

2. A compound defined in claim 1 in the form of the acetic acid salt.

3. A compound having the structural formula

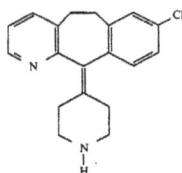

or a pharmaceutically acceptable salt thereof.

4. A compound having the structural formula

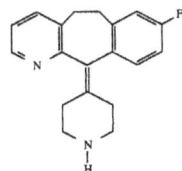

or a pharmaceutically acceptable salt thereof.

5. An antihistaminic pharmaceutical composition which comprises an antihistaminic effective amount of a compound as defined in claim 1 in combination with a pharmaceutically acceptable carrier.

6. An antihistaminic pharmaceutical composition which comprises an antihistaminic effective amount of the compound defined in claim 2 in combination with a pharmaceutically acceptable carrier.

7. An antihistaminic pharmaceutical composition which comprises an antihistaminic effective amount of the compound defined in claim 3 in combination with a pharamaceutically acceptable carrier.

8. An antihistaminic pharmaceutical composition which comprises an antihistaminic effective amount of the compound defined in claim 4 in combination with a pharmaceutically acceptable carrier.

9. A composition as defined in claim 7 in unit dosage form.

10. A composition as defined in claim 8 in unit dosage form.

11. A transdermally acceptable pharmaceutical composition comprising an anti-allergic effective amount of a compound as defined in claim 1 and a pharmaceutically acceptable transdermal carrier.

12. A transdermally acceptable pharamaceutical composition comprising a anti-allergic effective amount of a compound as defined in claim 3 and a pharmaceutically acceptable transdermal carrier.

13. A transdermally acceptable pharamaceutical composition comprising an anti-allergic effective amount of a compound as defined in claim 4 and a pharmaceutically acceptable transdermal carrier.

14. A method for treating allergic reactions in a mammal which comprises administering to said mammal an anti-allergic effective amount of a compound as defined in claim 1.

15. A method of treating allergic reactions in a mammal which comprises administering to said mammal an anti-allergic effective amount of a compound as defined in claim 3.

16. A method for treating allergic reactions in a mammal which comprises administering to said mammal an anti-allergic effective amount of a compound as defined in claim 4.

Figure 3: Patent 4,659,716 claims. *Source: USPTO*

4,659,716. The first claim sets a broad and well-defined scope. It shows the basic chemical formula of the protected compound and also claims "... a pharmaceutical acceptable salt thereof ..." while mentioning two specific derivatives. Claims 2-4 provide specific examples extending from the first claim. Claim 2 claims an acetic acid salt, claim 3 describes a chlorinated derivative, and claim 4 describes a fluorinated derivative.

Claims 5-10 are composition claims which describe the active drug compound as a combination in various therapeutic form. Claims 11-13 specifically describe transdermal dosage options and further refine the invention to usage for treatment of allergies. Finally, claims 14-16 focus on the method-of-use, claiming treatment of allergies regardless of dosage form.

These claims overlap and cover derivatives of the key drug compound in complementary ways. The likely rationale for this redundancy is to balance generality and specificity. From a commercial perspective it is advantageous for a patent to claim the largest possible scope. The combination of broad claims and specific claims provides the potential for broad protection, while providing fallback positions in the event that some claims are invalidated.

COMMON PATENT CLAIM TYPES

Patent claims can roughly divided into several categories. Understanding these categories can provide a shorthand for gauging the ability of a patent to block the launch of similar drugs. There are dozens of claim types; this section describes some of the more common types.

Compound Claims

Claims describing active ingredient in a drug are generally regarded as the strongest type of patent claims. Because generic drugs must contain the same active ingredient as a branded drug, it is not possible to develop a generic without infringing on a well-written compound claim.

Claims 1, 3, and 4 in the Claritin patent above are examples of compound claims.

Process Claims

In cases where a drug compound is naturally-occurring, it may be necessary to patent the purification procedures rather than the compound itself. Even if a drug is novel, it may still be useful to patent the production methods.

Product-by-process claims are similar to process claims, but they are used in special cases such as when a product defies description and can only be defined by the process by which it is made.

A downside to patenting production methods is that their disclosure may facilitate generic competition once a patent expires. If a drug is sufficiently complicated to manufacture it may be preferable to keep the manufacturing processes as trade secrets (See the example of Premarin in the section on *Trade Secrets*, in the chapter on *Patents and Other Forms of Intellectual Property Protection*). Also, if another company can find an economically-attractive alternative production method that falls outside the scope of the patented claims, then the process patent may be unable to exclude them from the market.

Formulation and Dosage Claims

Beyond patenting the active drug compound and the purification and manufacturing methods it is also possible to patent the dosage form. Examples of claimed dosage forms include extended-release capsules, transdermal patches, or solutions for injection.

Dosage form claims are sometimes called formulation claims, and this name highlights an important consideration in obtaining a patent; it cannot be obvious. Simply dissolving an orally-dosed pill and putting in a syringe is unlikely to be patentable without evidence of substantial challenges overcome in making the new dosage form work.

Use Claims

It is also possible to claim the use of a drug. For drugs with a single indication use claims can effectively keep generics off the market. Should a drug have more than one indication, then generics may be able to launch under a *skinny label* and gain approval only for unpatented indications. This strategy is often used with the hope that physicians will prescribe a less-expensive generic off label for an indication covered by a more expensive patent-protected branded drug.

Claims 5-16 of the Claritin patent above include mention of application as an anti-histamine in general with specific mention of treating allergic reactions.

EXPIRED PATENTS

Patents are designed to communicate knowledge. Indeed, similar to journal articles patents can serve as a form of technical literature. A vital difference between patents and journal articles, however, is that patents are not peer-reviewed for scientific accuracy.

Expired patents can be valuable sources of information even after they expire. They can advance research by enabling new research to build on prior efforts. Medicinal chemists working on developing new drugs or generic drugs can look to expired patents to copy or improve on previously-patented techniques.

One of the criteria for patent grants is that an invention not be obvious. Accordingly, patents may provide detailed details of prior failed attempts to solve a problem, to build a case for non-obviousness. This can help other researchers avoid following paths which eluded others, or it can arm them with knowledge to work around the failures of others. Furthermore, if a technology already exists and is available in the public domain due to patent expiration, then the opportunity for significant R&D savings may exist.

PATENT LITIGATION

PATENT CHALLENGES

The ANDA process establishes filing for generic approval of a patented drug as an act of "artificial infringement." This definition serves the interests of both innovator and generic drug companies.

Without clarifying that filing an application constitutes infringement, branded companies would potentially need to wait until a generic drug launched, and damages had accrued, before they could engage in litigation. By enabling branded drug makers to litigate their patents before the generic drug is actually marketed, the branded company doesn't need to suffer damages. Generic firms likewise benefit because they are often able to resolve patent disputes before launch (infringement gives them *standing* to challenge a patent), preventing them from having to compensate innovators for damages.

Resolving patent issues before launch provides clarity for distributors, pharmacies, and patients alike. Knowing that patent issues have been addressed can give them more certainty that there will be a consistent supply of generic drugs.

District Courts and Patent Trial and Appeal Board

Before the Leahy–Smith America Invents Act (AIA) was enacted the most common way to challenge the validity of patents was for a party at risk of being found guilty of patent infringement to challenge the patent in district courts. The requirement for a patent challenger to have standing meant that a generic company had to wait until it was sued, or risked being sued, for patent infringement before a patent challenge could be initiated. In 2012 the AIA established an *inter partes* review (IPR) pathway to challenge patents. Because the PTAB does not have a standing requirement, under IPR any party can question the validity of a patent.

There are some fundamental differences between IPRs and district court litigation. Firstly, the standard of proof of invalidity in an IPR is lower than that used in district courts. In district courts the plaintiff must demonstrate *clear and compelling evidence* of noninfringement or invalidity. For IPRs the burden of proof for invalidity is the *preponderance of the evidence.*

A second difference is that the PTAB cannot address patent infringement. Noninfringement of patents can only be introduced in district court cases. Also, IPR invalidity challenges are limited to obviousness and anticipation based on prior art patents and publications. District court litigation is more appropriate for invalidity arguments not predicated on prior art.

THE BIOSIMILAR PATENT DANCE

Just as the *Orange Book* lists all the FDA approved small-molecule drugs and the patents which must be addressed prior to ANDA approval, there exists a compendium of biologic drugs. The *Purple Book*, formally known as *Lists of Licensed Biological Products with Reference Product Exclusivity and Biosimilarity or Interchangeability Evaluations*, includes the date a biologic was licensed (approved), if it has reference product exclusivity, and its biosimilar/interchangeable status.

Importantly, no patents are listed. That means that unlike small-molecules there is no patent linkage for biologics; biosimilar entrants must independently identify blocking patents.

The *patent dance* is the name given to the method by which potential patent disputes between branded biologic companies and biosimilar entrants are resolved. For generic small-molecule drugs the Paragraph I-IV certification process (see *When can generics launch?* in the chapter *Innovative and Follower Drugs*) can address patent issues before launch. For biosimilars the applicant must notify the branded biologic manufacturer that they plan to market a competing product.

As with ANDA approval, this is an act of "artificial infringement", giving the branded company standing to sue the biosimilar entrant for patent infringement. If the branded firm elects to assert its patents against the biosimilar entrant, it can provide a list of all patents it believes are infringed.

The Biologics Price Competition and Innovation Act defines timelines under which both parties should exchange correspondence defining the patents protecting the drug and how their claims will or will not be infringed. This process sets the stage for formal litigation.

EXTRACTING INFORMATION FROM PATENT LITIGATION

Examining litigation can provide valuable intelligence for innovator and generic drug developers alike. Information which may be exposed in the course of litigation includes private settlement agreements, trade secrets, revenue statements, and more. Additionally legal budgets and litigation strategies can also be studied.

If a party does not take care to protect trade secrets which are disclosed in litigation, or if the courts deny efforts to prevent public access to litigation proceedings, then the trade secrets may be exposed. Additionally, if litigation centers on a previously-unpublished settlement agreement then the terms of that agreement may become publicly available. For example, the case study *Extracting Competitive Intelligence From Litigation* at the end of this book reveals budgets for patent litigation, licensing terms and revenues, and settlement terms which emerged in the course of litigation.

For popular drugs there are often a flurry of ANDAs Paragraph IV certifications filed at the earliest-available opportunity. Filing an ANDA early and winning a patent challenge introduces the potential for 180-day generic market exclusivity, which can be very lucrative. The downside to this approach is that if there are multiple first-day Paragraph IV filers, then they may end up sharing 180-day exclusivity. Fur-

US Court Litigation for RESTASIS

Glossary

Show 10 entries

EXCEL CSV

PATENT	CASE NAME	DOCKET	DATE FILED	DATE TERMINATED	CAUSE	COURT	JURY DEMAND	LINK TO DOCKET
8,629,111	TEVA PHARMACEUTICALS USA, INC. v. AZAR, II	1:18-cv-02304	2018-10-17		05:702 Administrative Procedure Act	District Court, District of Columbia	None	External link to docket
8,629,111	TEVA PHARMACEUTICALS USA, INC. v. AZAR, II	1:18-cv-02394-RDM	2018-10-17		05:702 Administrative Procedure Act	District Court, District of Columbia	None	External link to docket
8,629,111	Allergan, Inc. v. Amneal Pharmaceuticals LLC	1:18-cv-01457	2018-09-20		35:271 Patent Infringement	District Court, D. Delaware	Plaintiff	External link to docket

Figure 4: Restatis patent litigation. *Source: DrugPatentWatch*

thermore, these first patent challengers lack the opportunity to study prior patent challenges.

Using litigation histories to study the strategies of patent challengers and defendants can also help innovators draft stronger patents. Some generic companies prefer to focus on opportunities where first-round challengers have failed. By waiting until others have lost patent infringement cases it is possible to study those challenges and to develop new arguments.

WRITE BETTER PATENTS

Just as studying failed patent challenges can help a generic company learn from the efforts of prior challengers, innovators can also learn from patent challenges. While the primary goal of patent prosecution is to obtain a patent grant, a granted patent is of little value if it cannot stand up to challenge.

Accordingly, attorneys involved in drafting and prosecuting patents are advised to study patent litigation to anticipate patent challenges and to produce stronger litigation-resistant patents. For example, if a company is seeking patent protection for a new dosage form (e.g. making an oral drug available through a transdermal patch) or for a modification to an existing drug (e.g. making an extended-release for-

Transdermal Patch Drugs

Glossary

Show 10 entries EXCEL CSV

APPLICANT	TRADENAME	GENERIC NAME	DOSAGE	NDA	APPROVAL DATE	TE	TYPE	RLD	RS	PATENT NO.	PATENT EXPIRATION	PRODUCT
Scilex Pharms Inc	ZTLIDO	lidocaine	PATCH;TOPICAL	207962-001	Feb 28, 2018		RX	Yes	Yes	9,283,174	2031-05-10	Y
Scilex Pharms Inc	ZTLIDO	lidocaine	PATCH;TOPICAL	207962-001	Feb 28, 2018		RX	Yes	Yes	9,925,264	2031-05-10	Y
Scilex Pharms Inc	ZTLIDO	lidocaine	PATCH;TOPICAL	207962-001	Feb 28, 2018		RX	Yes	Yes	9,931,403	2031-05-10	Y
Hisamitsu Pharm Co	SALONPAS	menthol; methyl salicylate	PATCH;TOPICAL	022029-001	Feb 20, 2008		OTC	Yes	Yes	8,809,615	2030-01-03	Y

Figure 5: Transdermal patch drug patents. *Source: DrugPatentWatch*

mulation), they can examine prior patents covering similar modifications.

Reading granted patents can help aid in developing claims which are unlikely to be declared obvious by a patent examiner. By studying tactics by which prior generic or 505(b)(2) entrants were able to work around claims is may also be possible to draft better claims which are difficult for other companies to circumvent. Studying litigation can also reveal the structure and content of claims which have successfully prevailed in invalidity challenges.

EXPORTING SUCCESSFUL PATENT CHALLENGES

Because of the size of the U.S. biopharmaceutical market and the strong incentives for generic companies to challenge patents on branded drugs, the majority of patent challenges are anticipated to occur first in the U.S.

While patent laws and enforceability differ between countries, it is worth following U.S. patent litigation to see if successful patent challenges can be extended to other countries.

Market Size and Quality

For branded and generic drugs alike it is vital to distinguish between market size and market quality. Depending on a company's structure and goals the quality of a market may be as important, or more important than how innovative a new drug is or how large the market is. For example, some companies may be able to compete effectively in a large and crowded market whereas others are better suited for smaller markets with fewer alternatives.

The nature of a drug and the disease(s) it treats can influence the quality of a market. A drug meeting a significant need for a relatively small population may warrant a higher unit price than a non-essential drug serving a larger population. Drugs serving small, focused, audiences may also benefit from reduced marketing and distribution costs. These drugs may be best-suited for small companies with correspondingly small salesforces and management teams. For a larger company, niche drugs may fail to fully utilize the company's resources or to attract sufficient attention from management.

PREVALENCE, PRESENTATION, AND PRESCRIPTION

Three important factors in defining the market for a drug are the prevalence of the target disease(s), the frequency with which patients present to physicians with relevant conditions, and the number of prescriptions which are ultimately filled.

Ultimately, drug developers only earn revenues when prescriptions are filled. So for conditions which may be prevalent but for which patients are unaware that they are afflicted, such as hypertension, the relatively low rates of patients going to physicians and being diagnosed can create a substantial gap between the number of individuals who have the condition and the number of drugs being prescribed. Similarly, if a drug treating a non-critical condition has unpleasant side-effects then patients may elect not to fill (or renew) their prescriptions.

For branded drugs competition is generally in the form of alternate treatments, each of which may fundamentally different characteristics. For example, Figure 1 shows approved anticholestermic agents. Some of these drugs are patented, and others have generic competition.

These approved drugs can be used to model sales projections for any new anticholestermic drug. The patent expirations of these drugs and the potential for brand-extensions should also be considered in anticipating changes in the competitive landscape for any new entrant.

Anticholesteremic Agents

Show 10 entries

Glossary

EXCEL CSV

APPLICANT	TRADENAME	GENERIC NAME	DOSAGE	NDA	APPROVAL DATE	TE	TYPE	RLD	RS	PATENT NO.	PATENT EXPIRATION	PRODUCT	SUBSTANCE	DELIST REQ.	EXCLUSIVITY EXPIRATION
[illegible]	FLOLIPID	simvastatin	SUSPENSION;ORAL	206679-001	Apr 21, 2016		Rx	Yes	No	[illegible]	2030-02-23	Y			
[illegible]	FLOLIPID	simvastatin	SUSPENSION;ORAL	206679-002	Apr 21, 2016		Rx	Yes	Yes	[illegible]	2030-02-23	Y			
Msd Intl Gmbh	ZETIA	ezetimibe	TABLET;ORAL	021445-001	Oct 25, 2002	AB	Rx	Yes	Yes	7,612,058*PED	2026-04-30			Y	

Figure 1: Approved anticholesteremic agents. *Source: DrugPatentWatch*

REVENUES

Historic drug sales data can help with market sizing. By examining sales trends you can gauge the attractiveness of the market entry.

For example, Figure 2 shows a decreasing trend in the number of units of Premarin sold over time, indicating a shift in prescribing trends towards other treatments. Generic entrants should carefully consider entering a market with declining sales.

In considering a 505(b)(2) application to potentially improve on drug shortcomings it would be prudent to take a deeper look at the pharmacodynamics of the drug (e.g. can a new formulation address side-effects or peak/trough issues).

In contrast with the declining sales for Premarin, Figure 3 shows increasing sales of Lantus, showing strength both for the category and for the drug.

These growing sales make a compelling case for entry of branded drugs and followers alike.

CHANNELS

Beyond sales volumes and trends it is important to gain information on sales channels. Knowing which sales channels

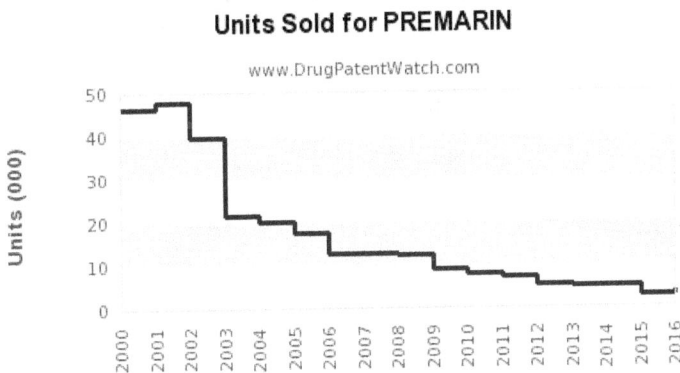

Figure 2: Premarin units sold over time. *Source: DrugPatentWatch*

Sales Revenues for LANTUS

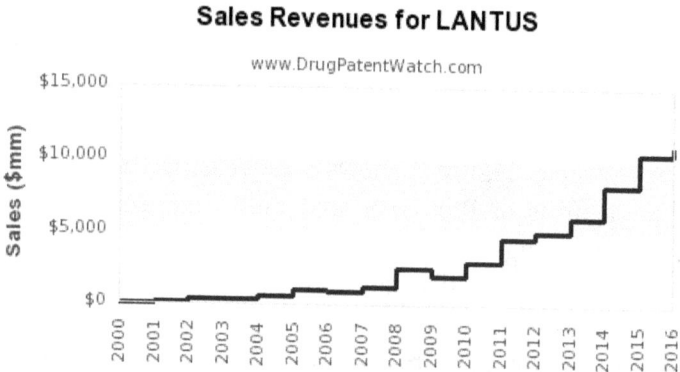

Figure 3: Lantus sales over time. *Source: DrugPatentWatch*

are dominant for a given drug can help you assess alignment with your business model and commercial relationships, and this knowledge can also help you develop tactical partnerships to gain an edge on competitors.

The U.S. is the world's largest drug market, and it is also the least regulated in terms of price. However, the majority of drugs sold in the U.S. are sold directly or indirectly to the government through Medicare Part D, Medicaid, and other programs. Furthermore, payers base their formulary inclusion decisions on a number of factors, including clinical outcomes and the cost of a treatment relative to other options.

This means that even in the absence of formal price controls, manufacturers in the U.S. still face significant political and marketplace pressure to keep prices down. Payers can use a variety of methods, such as formulary exclusion, co-payment tiers, and preferred status.

Patients may also pay for drugs out-of-pocket, which introduces an additional set of marketing and positioning constraints.

Evaluation of the which payers ultimately pay for prescriptions, and what volume of revenues is attributed to each, can yield vital information to support portfolio management and prioritization.

For example, Viagra and sildenafil (generic Viagra) have markedly different sales channels. As shown in Figure 4, the majority (43%) of Viagra revenues are derived from drugs paid for out-of-pocket by patients or family members. Further, Figure 5 shows that more than 25% of Viagra revenues come from mail-order sales and nearly 50% come from pharmacies inside other stores.

One might assume that the branded and generic versions of a drug will demonstrate similar sales distribution, but for sildenafil that is not the case. As shown in Figure 6 neatly 50% of generic revenues stem from Medicare. Further, as shown in Figure 7 fewer than 1% of revenues are derived from mail-order. These trends suggest that strict generic switching policies are employed by Medicare, and that mail-order buyers have low price sensitivity and strong brand affinity.

The sales channels, as described above, are important

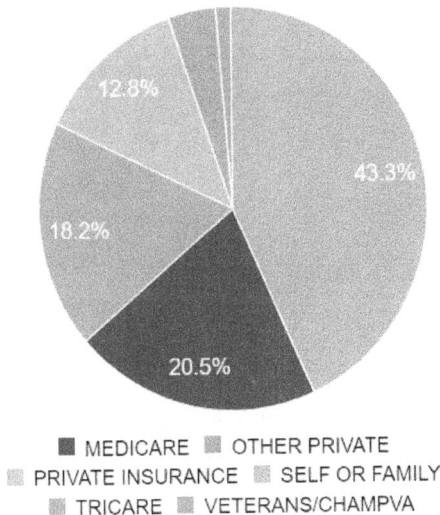

VIAGRA Revenues by Payment Method

MEDICARE   OTHER PRIVATE
PRIVATE INSURANCE   SELF OR FAMILY
TRICARE   VETERANS/CHAMPVA

Figure 4: Viagra payment methods. *Source: DrugPatentWatch*

VIAGRA Revenues by Pharmacy Type

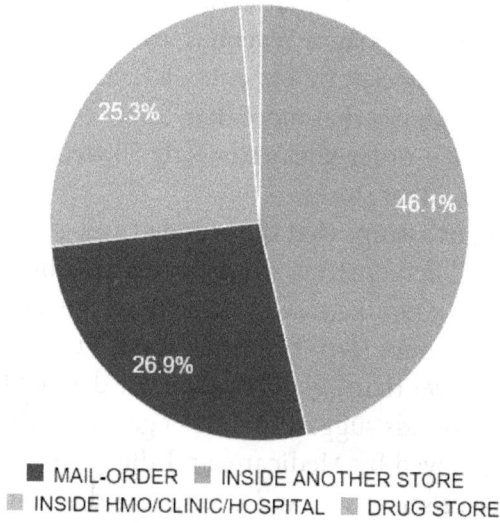

- MAIL-ORDER   INSIDE ANOTHER STORE
- INSIDE HMO/CLINIC/HOSPITAL   DRUG STORE

Figure 5: Viagra sales channels. *Source: DrugPatentWatch*

SILDENAFIL CITRATE Revenues by Payment Method

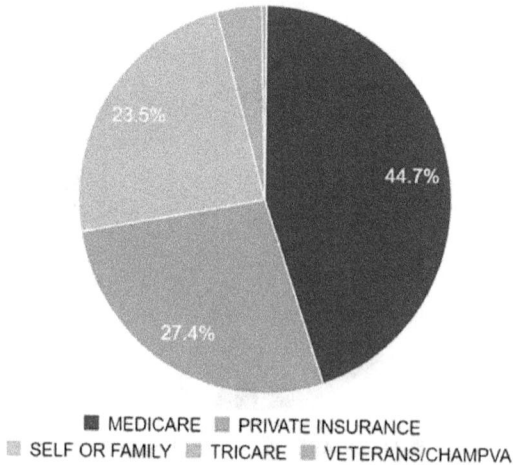

- MEDICARE   PRIVATE INSURANCE
- SELF OR FAMILY   TRICARE   VETERANS/CHAMPVA

Figure 6: Sildenafil payment methods. *Source: DrugPatentWatch*

SILDENAFIL CITRATE Revenues by Pharmacy Type

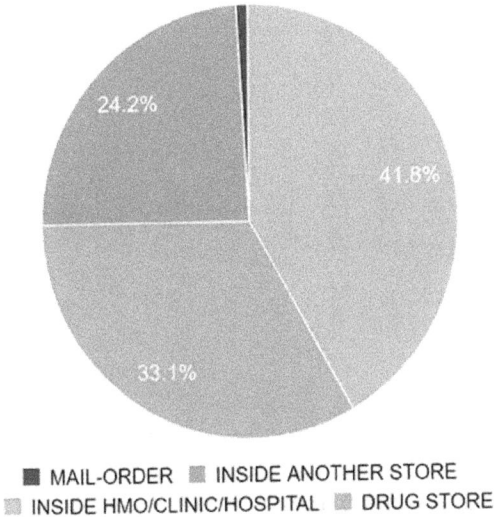

Figure 7: Sildenafil sales channels. *Source: DrugPatentWatch*

factors in understanding the path to market. The payer distribution will impact important factors such as price sensitivity, the opportunity for long-term contracts, and the need to adjust pricing or provide discounts. These factors also interface with sales volumes. For example a drug addressing a significant unmet need for a small patient population will likely amount to a small portion of expenditures by institutional payers, avoiding price pressures.

DRUG PRICES

GENERIC COMPETITION

A quick and simple way to gauge brand strength and generic competition is to look at the relative prices of branded and generic drugs. Figure 8 shows some of the branded drugs

Top Branded vs. Generic Drug Prices

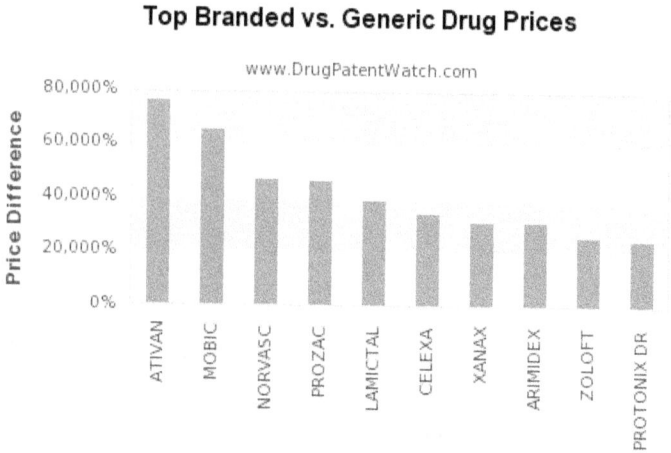

Figure 8: Branded vs. generic drug prices. *Source: DrugPatentWatch*

with the greatest markups over generics.

Drugs with small branded vs. generic price differences (i.e. generics sell for nearly the same price as branded drugs) may represent strong generic entry opportunities. In these cases it is worth examining the number of generic suppliers and investigating why generic competition has not driven prices down.

When branded vs generic drugs show broad price differences (i.e. generics are selling at a strong discount to branded drugs) one should exercise caution before electing to enter those markets. The large price difference may indicate extensive generic competition and the presence of many suppliers. A new entrant may find it challenging to capture substantial market share. A better approach in these cases may be a 505(b)(2) strategy to develop a drug with improved characteristics.

PRICE TRENDS

Trends in drug prices can also inform market entry decisions. For branded drugs the trends can help predict generic entry. For example because many branded drugs show price increases in advance of generic entry, a price increase coinciding with litigation may indicate that the brand is preparing for an adverse decision and the generic may be able to enter prior to the anticipated patent expiration date.

Trends in prices for branded drugs should be combined with unit sales (see *Revenues,* above) to indicate if the overall market is improving or declining. For generic drug prices the same consideration applies. In Figure 9 prices for dicyclomine demonstrate an upwards trend. This may indicate a good opportunity for market entry.

By contrast, Figure 10 shows a declining trend in azetazolamide prices, which suggests increasing competition or decreasing market demand — both of which would reduce the commercial attractiveness of launching a competiting branded drug or a generic drug.

Price trends and unit sales can also help evaluate the

Figure 9: Dicyclomine drug price trends. *Source: DrugPatentWatch*

Price Trends for ACETAZOLAMIDE

Figure 10: Acetazolamide drug price trends. *Source: DrugPatentWatch*

commercial potential of a therapeutic class. If the majority of drugs in a therapeutic class demonstrate the same directional trend, it can suggest favorable or weak indications for branded and generic entry alike.

PROJECTING GENERIC PRICES AND REVENUES

After ranking portfolio candidates it is important to also find prices which buyers will find attractive. Pharmacy pricing information can be combined with federal pricing to bracket the top- and bottom-ranges for new entrants.

Figure 11 shows the average price pharmacies pay for atorvastatin (generic Lipitor). These prices combine reports from large and small pharmacies, and they include discounts, which means that they tend to be slightly lower than the average wholesale price (AWP) reported by other sources.

The average pharmacy cost data can be complemented by federal pricing. Because federal clients must, by law, receive the best available prices for drugs, federal drug costs are a good surrogate for what large national chains pay for drugs.

Average Pharmacy Cost for ATORVASTATIN

These are average pharmacy acquisition costs (net of discounts) from a US national survey

Glossary

EXCEL   CSV

Show 10 ▾ entries

DRUG NAME	NDC	PRICE/UNIT ($)	UNIT	DATE
ATORVASTATIN 10 MG TABLET	00093-5056-98	0.05618	EACH	2018-10-17
ATORVASTATIN 10 MG TABLET	00093-5056-98	0.04991	EACH	2019-04-17
ATORVASTATIN 80 MG TABLET	00093-5057-98	0.14853	EACH	2018-05-22
ATORVASTATIN 80 MG TABLET	00093-5057-98	0.14429	EACH	2019-02-20

Figure 11: Average price for atorvastatin. *Source: DrugPatentWatch*

Average Pharmacy Cost vs. Best Drug Price Differences

These prices are derived from two data sources which used different methodologies. Despite best efforts to align the data, some discrepancies may remain

EXCEL   CSV

Show 10 ▾ entries

DRUG NAME	AVERAGE PHARMACY COST ($)	BEST PRICE ($)	DIFFERENCE ($)	DIFFERENCE (%)	BEST PRICE VENDOR
MORPHINE SO4	0.32204	0.01420	0.30784	2,167.85	West-Ward Pharmaceuticals Corporation
PROPARACAINE	1.89856	0.08333	1.80523	2,165.36	Sandoz, Inc.
GALANTAMINE HYDROBROMIDE	1.52919	0.06800	1.46119	2,149.81	Johnson & Johnson Health Care Systems, Inc. obo Patriot Pharm
HYDROCHLOROTHIAZIDE	0.46519	0.02100	0.44419	2,115.19	Greenstone, Ltd.
ONGLYZA	13.24472	0.60000	12.64472	2,107.45	AstraZeneca Pharmaceuticals LP

Figure 12: Average vs. best drug prices. *Source: DrugPatentWatch*

So, by combining the average pharmacy costs with the federal costs it is possible to roughly bracket the upper- and lower-ranges of prices of a drug. This valuable information can help smooth a drug launch.

Branded Drugs

Market entry strategies for branded drugs, for generic drugs, and for 505(b)(2) hybrids are fundamentally different. This section addresses considerations specific to branded drugs, many of which also apply to 505(b)(2) drugs as well.

MARKET SIZE

One of the primary considerations for branded and generic drugs alike is the size of the market.

For generic entry market size estimates can be based on the financial performance of the branded drugs they are copying. Unlike novel branded drugs, however, each generic drug will likely face competition from fully-substitutable alternatives. Accordingly, estimating the share of market that a generic will command may be based on the quality and quantity of competitors. For branded drugs market share may be easier to predict, but estimating the market size can be far more complicated.

Figures 1 and 2 expand on the discussion in the chapter on *Market Size and Quality*, by illustrating the impact of drug prices and drug spending on availability of drugs.

Figure 1 shows that for countries with lower drug prices, the number of drugs available in that country are fewer, and

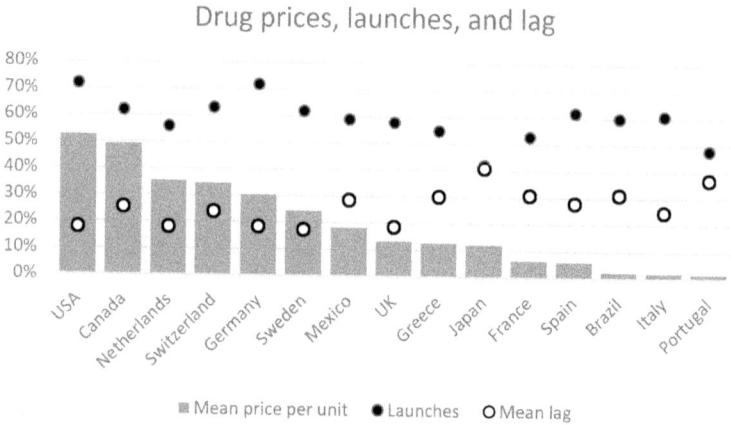

Figure 1: Drug prices, launches, and lag. *Source: Danzon and Epstein, (2008) Effects of regulation on drug launch and pricing in interdependent markets. NBER Working Paper 14041*

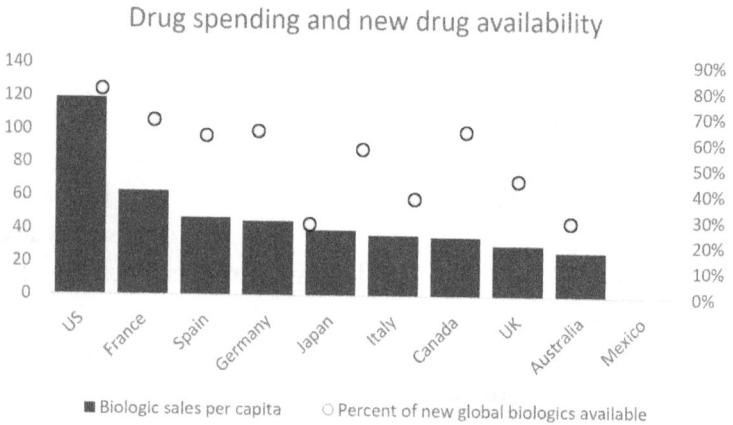

Figure 2: Drug spending and new drug availability. *Source: Danzon, P.M. and Furukawa, M.F. (2006) Prices And Availability Of Biopharmaceuticals: An International Comparison. Health Affairs 25(5) pp.1353-1362*

the lag before a drug receives approval in that country (presumably due to later application for approval) is greater.

Figure 2 echoes the sentiments of Figure 1, but instead of measuring the price of drugs it examines spending on drugs. As with Figure 1, when spending on drugs decreases (potentially because of a smaller market, or because of lower prices) the availability of drugs decreases.

The trend between drug prices, drug spending, and market availability clearly has implications for national policies. It also suggests that when prioritizing drugs in development in a single market, the leads likely to generate higher revenues will be favored.

As described in the chapter on *Market Size and Quality*, one way to estimate market size for new drugs is to look at historic data for similar drugs already on the market. A problem remains for estimating market sizes for first-in-class drugs and, unfortunately, textbooks are replete with examples of estimates gone wrong.

Exubera presents an example of what can happen when estimates are too optimistic. Exubera was launched as a first-in-class inhalable version of insulin in a partnership between Pfizer and Nektar Therapeutics. Pfizer's strength in drug development and marketing was to complement Nektar Therapeutics' dry powder aerosol technology.

The drug was originally hailed as the most significant innovation in diabetes treatment in decades, and despite sales projections in the billions of dollars, Exubera was pulled by Pfizer one year after launch.

In discontinuing the drug, Pfizer cited long-term safety concerns, the need for extensive patient training, and patient reluctance to use the cumbersome and conspicuous inhalation device. Pfizer took a $2.8 billion loss after posting only $12 million in Exubera sales. Nektar eliminated more than 100 jobs and announced a "transition form a drug delivery service provider to a therapeutics drug development organization."

The case of Immunex's first-in-class rheumatoid arthritis drug Enbrel illustrates that underestimating demand can also have negative consequences. The drug far-exceeded Immunex's estimated sales projections and it set a 24-month growth record for biotechnology drugs. When demand far outstripped supply Immunex had to resort to rationing the drug.

Immunex's low estimates were based on the drug's high price and targeting for patients with severe arthritis. However, once patients started seeing dramatic improvements, news of the drug spread and demand escalated rapidly. The inability to meet demand caused Immunex's stock price to drop and they were ultimately acquired by Amgen.

MARKET PROTECTION AND COMPETITION

Beyond market size it is also important to consider patent protection, regulatory exclusivity, and other market protections. With strong patent protection or regulatory exclusivity a company can be assured that they will not have any direct competitors. Softer forms of market protection, such as manufacturing patents, can give a company a financial advantage over competitors, but not provide absolute exclusivity.

Despite not fully excluding competitors, partial market protection can still provide advantages such as reduced manufacturing costs or preferred relationships with downstream partners. Many of the tactics described in *Lifecycle Management*, below, also apply to situations where a company must share a market.

STRATEGIC ALIGNMENT

There is considerable stratification in the pharmaceutical and biotechnology sectors. Large companies may require a threshold market size to consider market entry, and smaller firms may define their focus based on niche markets, technical opportunities, or disease categories. For example, companies may specialize in making orally-dosed drugs available in alternative dosage forms for patients with difficulty swallowing. Their prioritization criteria may favor leveraging their dosage-form platform over ensuring broad market dominance.

Likewise, a company specializing in selling through hospital pharmacies, mail-order/Internet pharmacies, or government contracts may use their established sales channels to exclude competitors

For example, many chemotherapy drugs are administered in the physician's office. This means that prescription decisions may be based on incentives for physicians rather than incentives for pharmacists. If two drugs differ in the number of patient visits required, or in other factors which can influence physician workload without increasing revenues, then the drug better aligned with physician's interests may receive preferential prescription.

Beyond market sizing it is also important to gain input from the downstream stakeholders. For example, clinicians, payers and other parties should be consulted to determine if a drug aligns with their objectives.

Discussions with payers can help evaluate the likelihood that a drug will be reimbursed. If a drug will not be reimbursed, then it is unlikely to succeed in the marketplace. Additional research may be required to demonstrate improved clinical outcomes or opportunities for cost-savings.

Physicians actively prescribing medicines for the targeted condition can provide input on prescription patterns (e.g. do patients take a drug only once; do they refill their prescriptions, do they regularly switch drugs) and how each drug compares with other medications for the same indication. If these opinions contradict research findings they can identify potential weaknesses in the research, or opportunities for marketing and education.

TRACKING DRUGS IN DEVELOPMENT

Figure 3 shows clinical trials for MK-1775, a drug in development. Examining these trials, their progress, and their outcomes can help observers gauge the likely indications a com-

Figure 3: Clinical trial progress for MK-1775. *Source: DrugPatentWatch*

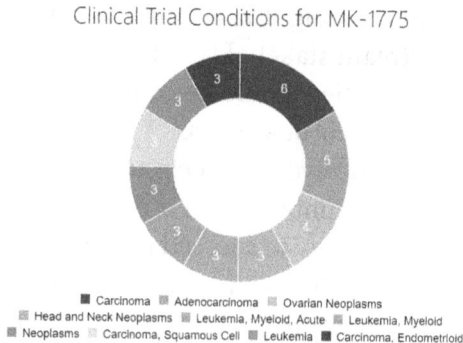

Clinical Trial Conditions for MK-1775

■ Carcinoma ■ Adenocarcinoma ▨ Ovarian Neoplasms
▨ Head and Neck Neoplasms ■ Leukemia, Myeloid, Acute ■ Leukemia, Myeloid
■ Neoplasms ▨ Carcinoma, Squamous Cell ■ Leukemia ■ Carcinoma, Endometrioid

Figure 4: Summary of therapeutic indications tested for MK-1775. *Source: DrugPatentWatch*

pany will target with their NDA. The conditions evaluated in clinical trials are summarized in Figure 4. Examination of other drugs being prescribed on-label and off-label for these indications can help build a robust models for the drug developer and for other parties.

A drug developer can use information on competing drugs in each therapeutic indication along with their therapeutic benefit, the revenues, and the number of patented and unpatented drugs (and projected patent expirations) to either guide clinical trials towards the diseases for which the drug will have the greatest benefit over existing alternatives and which also present strong market opportunities. Investors can also monitor clinical trials to evaluate opportunities to invest in the developing firm, in partners with ownership of the patent(s), or in companies assisting with clinical trials. Likewise, potential development, distribution, and manufacturing partners can follow clinical trial progress to find business opportunities.

Payers also have an interest in drugs in development. Beyond looking at clinical trials to identify new drugs in development which may provide money-saving alternatives to existing drugs, or other opportunities to reduce healthcare costs, it is also important to evaluate the potential loss-of-exclusivity dates so budgetary projections can anticipate possible generic entry. Figure 5 shows granted patents claiming MK-1775. The titles suggest the composition patent may

US Patents for MK-1775

DRUGNAME	PATENT NUMBER	PATENT TITLE	PATENT ASSIGNEE	ESTIMATED EXPIRATION
MK-1775	8,844,752	Block copolymers for stable micelles	Intezyne Technologies, Inc. (Tampa, FL)	2036-03-19
MK-1775	9,777,535	Methods for treating cancer using TOR kinase inhibitor combination therapy comprising administering substituted pyrazolo[2,3-b]pyridines	Signal Pharmaceuticals, LLC (San Diego, CA)	2035-04-15
MK-1775	8,653,092	Compositions and methods for treating cancer	Merck Sharp & Dohme Corp. (Rahway, NJ)	2031-11-22
MK-1775	9,309,186	Preparation of crystalline forms of dihydropyrazolopyrimidinone	Merck Sharp & Dohme Corp. (Rahway, NJ)	2034-03-08
MK-1775	8,546,375	Compositions and methods for treating cancer	Merck Sharp & Dohme Corp. (Rahway, NJ)	2032-06-11
MK-1775	8,791,125	Dihydropyrazolopyrimidinone derivatives	MSD K.K. (Chiyoda-Ku, Tokyo, JP)	2031-02-27

Figure 5: Patents claiming MK-1775. *Source: DrugPatentWatch*

expire in 2033; a deeper look at the patent claims and consideration of potential approved indications and patent term extensions can develop a stronger projection of potential generic entry of this drug.

LIFECYCLE MANAGEMENT

When patents and regulatory protections expire generic drugs are free to enter the market. The entry of multiple ge-

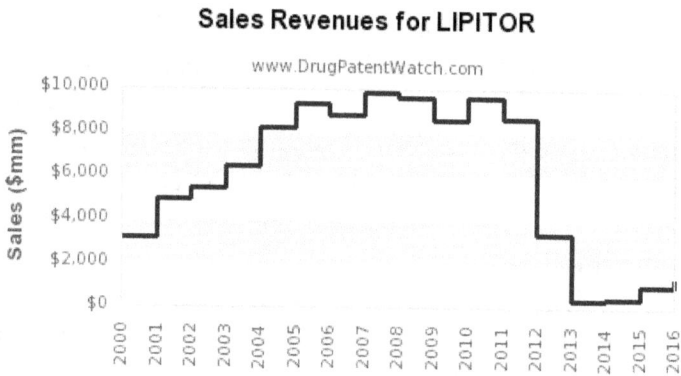

Figure 6: Lipitor patent cliff. *Source: DrugPatentWatch*

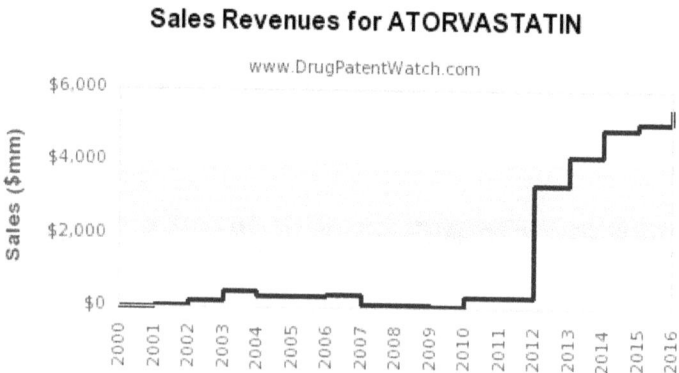

Figure 7: Atorvastatin sales climb after Lipitor patents expire. *Source: DrugPatentWatch*

neric versions of drugs can bring price competition, which can lead to precipitous decreases in revenues for branded drugs. Figure 6 shows how U.S. sales for Lipitor dropped by more than 90% shortly following generic entry. Figure 7 shows the simultaneous rapid growth of atorvastatin (generic Lipitor) sales.

In cases such as this, brands can lose billions of dollars in revenues in short order, as generic firms share a multi-billion dollar opportunity. With so much money at stake, innovative firms have strong incentives to extend branded sales as long as possible. This section describes many of the strategies and tactics used to protect revenues from branded drugs.

In implementing lifecycle management it is important to avoid violating antitrust and other marketplace laws. Overly aggressive tactics may result in punitive damages and even in criminal charges against company management.

STRATEGIC PRICING

Pricing is one of the simplest levers which can be used to maximize revenues from branded drugs.

One tactic to maintain branded sales is to lower prices to align more closely with generics. However, it is not uncommon for branded drug prices to increase before patent expiration. Knowing that price-sensitive buyers will switch to the generic, raising the branded drug price allows a company to maximize revenues from price-insensitive buyers. Rebates and other co-payment agreements can be combined with increased pricing to leverage and extend customer loyalty before widespread availability of generics.

BRANDING

Branding can be an effective complement to strategic pricing. For some drugs, especially those which are sold over-the-counter, branding can help maintain sales for many years after generic entry. Common pain relievers and allergy medicines demonstrate the power of branding. In most pharmacies branded pain-killers, allergy medicines, and others are sold alongside their branded counterparts. Despite assurances that the generic has passed FDA review and is fully substitutable with the brand, consumers frequently opt for the more-expensive branded versions of these drugs.

In another example, Viagra was so successfully branded during its patent-protected period that when consumers order from mail-order pharmacies they opt for Viagra over generic sildenafil (see *Channels* in the chapter on *Market Size and Quality*).

NEW THERAPEUTIC INDICATIONS

Finding new uses is a potent strategy to extend the commercial life of approved drugs. During initial clinical investigations, or in the process of monitoring post-approval patient outcomes, a company may find that a drug can address new conditions. Because the side-effects and pharmacokinetics of approved drugs are already known, the financial cost, timeline, and developmental risk of finding new indications for approved drugs is much less than for unproven compounds.

The application of a drug for secondary indications may also be patentable, allowing a branded drug to maintain strong sales even after generics launch for the first indication. Even if the secondary indications are unpatentable the new indications may still be able to obtain new clinical investigation exclusivity, preventing generic entry for three years.

An example of indication expansion is finasteride (see Figure 8). Merck first received approval for the drug under the brand name Proscar, to treat prostate enlargement. Later, when use for the treatment of hair loss was identified, Merck obtained new patents and gained approval for the new indi-

US Patents and Regulatory Information for FINASTERIDE

APPLICANT	TRADENAME	GENERIC NAME	DOSAGE	NDA	APPROVAL DATE	TE	TYPE	RLD	RS	PATENT NO.	PATENT EXPIRATION	PRODUCT	SUBSTANCE
Merck	PROSCAR	finasteride	TABLET;ORAL	020180-001	Jun 19, 1992	AB	RX	Yes	Yes				
Merck	PROPECIA	finasteride	TABLET;ORAL	020788-001	Dec 19, 1997	AB	RX	Yes	Yes				

Figure 8: Finasteride branded drugs from Merck. *Source: DrugPatentWatch*

cation under the brand name Propecia.

A caveat of filing for secondary indications is that generics may "carve-out" the patented indications and launch with labelling only for the original off-patent indication. This tactic is also called a "skinny label" or *Section viii* statement, after the relevant section of the Federal Food, Drug, and Cosmetic Act.

While skinny label generics cannot market the patented indications, they can launch in the hopes that physicians will recognize the opportunity to save their patience money and prescribe the generic drug *off-label*.

In the example of finasteride described above, Proscar was available in 5mg tablets and Propecia in 1mg tablets, complicating off-label prescription.

NEW FORMULATIONS

As with new indications, formulation changes may enable a branded drug to sustain sales even after generics launch. For example, formulating drugs into extended-release formulations may improve patient outcomes. For drugs with side-effects or therapeutic deficiencies related to *peaks* and *troughs* an extended release-formulation may enable a branded drug to be preferred over non-extended generics by payers and patients alike.

Similarly, switching dosage forms, such as making orally-dosed drugs available as transdermal patches for patients with trouble swallowing, can expand the market size for a drug.

Formulation improvements may be patentable, and they may also be opportunities for new clinical investigation exclusivity. An additional benefit of developing new formulations over obtaining approval for new indications is that generics may be blocked from the market for the new formulation.

If the new formulation is patented or protected by regulatory exclusivity, the generics will need to wait until loss of exclusivity.

NEW COMBINATIONS

If two drugs have complementary benefits it may make sense to combine them into a single dosage form. For example, after the patent on Prozac (fluoxetine) expired, Eli Lilly combined it with olanzapine to produce Symbyax. This combination of two drugs with activity as antidepressants was intended for treatment of patients who could not benefit from either drug alone.

As described in the chapter on *Patents and Other Forms of Intellectual Property Protection*, to be patentable inventions must be new and not obvious. So simply combining two complementary drugs is unlikely to be eligible for patent protection. The effect of combining the drugs should yield unexpected results.

Reimbursement and off-label use are also important factors. Payers tend to require that drugs yield better clinical outcomes than available alternatives. Also, if the constituents of a combination therapy are available off-patent, physicians will be free to individually prescribe the generic drug components instead of the patented, and likely more expensive, combination therapy.

Patent 6,960,577, which protected Symbyax, makes the

case for nonobviousness (emphasis added):

> The present invention provides the
> advantage of treatment of partial
> responding or refractory depres-
> sion with the atypical antipsychot-
> ics without the concomitant weight
> gain typically observed with such
> treatment, conferring a **marked and
> unexpected benefit** on the patient.

The impact of this combination was substantial. Prozac's patent protection expired in 2001, and the integration into Symbyax permitted patent-protected sales for refractory depression to continue through 2017.

ENANTIOMERS

Chemical molecules such as drugs can often exist in more than one structural form. A special case of structural variability is enantiomers, or mirror-image molecules. Just as your left and right hand are comprised of the same bones and the same joints, yet they are not identical, enantiomers are chemicals which are mirror-images of each other.

Many drugs contain more than one configuration of the same molecule. In the case of thalidomide, one enantiomer was therapeutically useful and the other produced birth defects. Thalidomide was never approved in the U.S., but after the dangerous side-effects were recognized it was withdrawn from the other markets in which it had received approval.

In cases where an inactive enantiomer has dangerous side-effects, undesirable side-effects, or even no measurable effect, there may be an opportunity to modify the production techniques to produce a higher proportion of the therapeutically-active enantiomer. Doing so can reduce the manufacturing cost of a drug, potentially enabling price competition with dual-enantiomer generics. If a branded drug can be profitably sold for only a small mark-up relative to generics then payers may defer substitution and continue to prefer the branded drug.

Single enantiomer drugs can improve therapeutic benefits, they can improve the side-effect profile, and they can also reduce the potential for negative drug-drug interactions. Beyond patenting purified enantiomer forms, single-enantiomer forms may also be eligible for 5-year new chemical entity regulatory exclusivity.

An example of a single-enantiomer drug is Nexium, which was developed from Prilosec. Prilosec is comprised of S- and R- forms of omeprazole (see Figure 9). With the patent for Prilosec expiring in 2002, AstraZeneca developed a single-enantiomer version, containing highly-purified esomeprazole. This drug was called Nexium and as can be seen in Figures 10 and 11 Nexium sales were able to more than compensate for the loss of Prilosec revenues after its patent expired.

OVER THE COUNTER

If drugs and the conditions they treat are safe enough for consumers to self-diagnose and select treatment options, the FDA may allow the drugs to be sold "over the counter" (OTC) rather than requiring a prescription.

OTC drugs tend to have stricter approval requirements than prescription drugs. The first consideration is to determine if the OTC drug is safe and effective when used without supervision. Because OTC drugs are likely to be used following self-diagnosis by patients, an otherwise safe drug may fail to obtain OTC approval simply because the underlying symptoms are similar to those which require physician intervention.

(S)-(-)-omeprazole (esomeprazole)   (R)-(+)-omeprazole

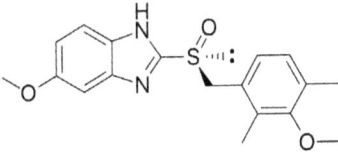

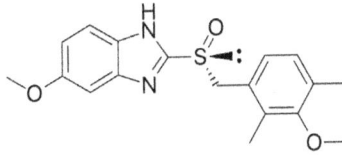

Figure 9: Omeprazole and esomeprazole. *Source: National Institutes of Health*

Sales Revenues for PRILOSEC

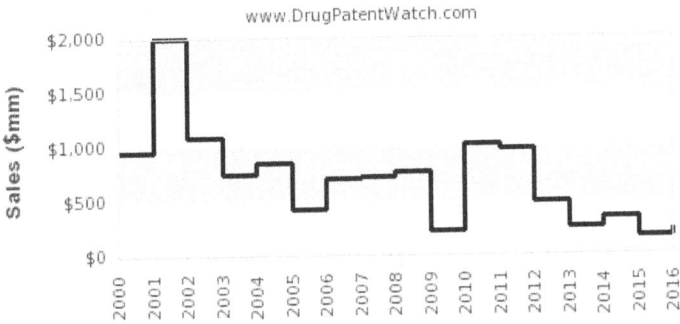

www.DrugPatentWatch.com

Figure 10: Prilosec sales. *Source: DrugPatentWatch*

Sales Revenues for NEXIUM

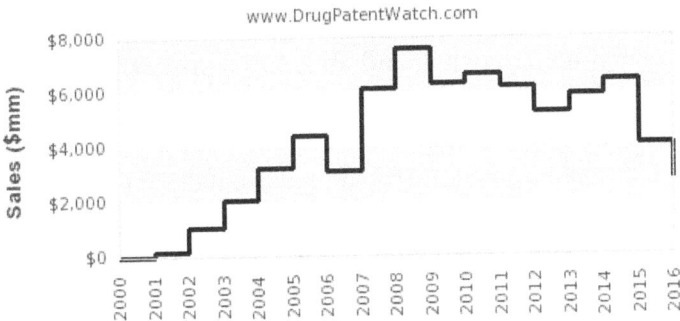

www.DrugPatentWatch.com

Figure 11: Nexium sales. *Source: DrugPatentWatch*

Sales Revenues for PRILOSEC OTC

Figure 12: Prilosec OTC sales. *Source: DrugPatentWatch*

Also, OTC drugs are liable to be used in the absence of any supervision, raising the possibility of use not in accordance with labeling.

As an incentive for making drugs available over the counter, if OTC approval requires new clinical testing the OTC drug may be eligible for three years of market exclusivity. One main benefit of OTC drugs is that they can have higher levels of sales for a longer duration of time. Branded companies may also be motivated to initiate an OTC-switch simply because they know that if they do not, a generic company may initiate a switch and obtain new clinical investigation exclusivity.

Building on the Prilosec example introduced in the above section on *Enantiomers*, AstraZeneca used an OTC switch of Prilosec in conjunction with the introduction of Nexium as part of a multi-channel approach to limit opportunities for generic competition (see Figure 12).

AUTHORIZED GENERICS

Brands facing patent expiration may elect to participate in the generic market themselves. Authorized generic drugs

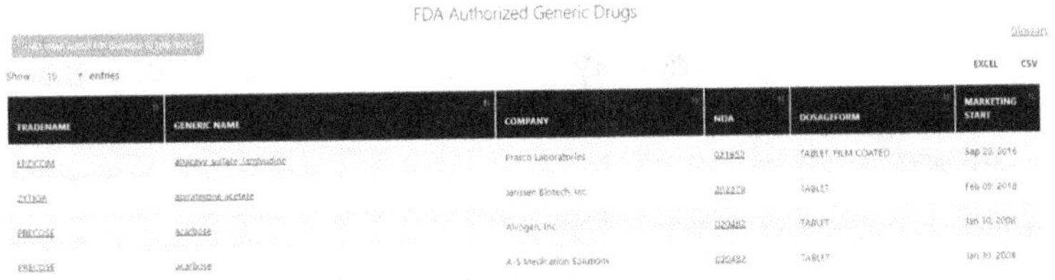
FDA Authorized Generic Drugs

Show 10 entries

EXCEL CSV

TRADENAME	GENERIC NAME	COMPANY	NDA	DOSAGEFORM	MARKETING START
EPZICOM	abacavir sulfate lamivudine	Prasco Laboratories	021652	TABLET, FILM COATED	Sep 29, 2016
ZYTIGA	abiraterone acetate	Janssen Biotech Inc	202379	TABLET	Feb 09, 2018
PRECOSE	acarbose	Alvogen Inc	020482	TABLET	Jan 10, 2008
PRECOSE	acarbose	A-S Medication Solutions	020482	TABLET	Jan 30, 2008

Figure 13: Authorized generic drugs. *Source: DrugPatentWatch*

are manufactured in the same facility as branded drugs, but are sold by a third party under a generic label. Unlike generic drugs, which must be approved under an ANDA and are manufactured by or for the ANDA applicant, authorized generics are the same as those approved under the original NDA, but instead of being sold by the NDA holder they are sold by an *authorized* generic company.

A common reason why brands may launch authorized generics is to increase competition in the generic market when other factors constrain the number of generic entrants. For example, if a generic company successfully invalidates a branded drug patent, they may be entitled to 180-day generic market exclusivity. With only two versions of a drug on the market — the original branded drug and the generic from the successful patent challenger — it is not uncommon for generic prices to be 80-90% of branded prices.

By launching an authorized generic drug, pressure can be applied to the generic with market exclusivity, compelling them to reduce their prices and negatively impacting the revenues they can gain during their 180-day exclusivity. Using the original drug's NDA to manufacture the authorized generic (it must use all the same approved procedures and facilities as the branded drug) enables it to work around the 180-day generic exclusivity period during which the FDA cannot approve another ANDA.

Another reason to launch an authorized generic is to take advantage of payer preferences. The first-to-market generic drug tends to benefit from extended market dominance. Further, payers may willfully pay a premium for authorized generics over other generics, knowing that the authorized generic is unlikely to suffer production shortages or bioequivalence issues.

Generic Entry

This chapter profiles the broad strategies and many of the tactics used by generic firms to find and prioritize generic entry opportunities. For a refresher on the conditions for generic entry you may want to look back at the chapter on *Innovative and Follower Drugs*.

Generic drugs are central to reducing the costs of medicine. They account for about 90% of the prescriptions dispensed in the USA, but only a quarter of drug spending. Part of the reason that generics are able to be sold at lower prices because generic companies have a much reduced research and development burden relative to innovators. Innovative firms spend years conducting expensive and failure-prone experimentation to discover potential drugs. These leads must then undergo exhaustive clinical trials to demonstrate their safety and efficacy. By contrast, generic companies can focus their efforts on drugs which have already been proven to be safe and effective. They can also cite the safety and efficacy of drugs that have already gained approval, avoiding costly animal and human clinical trials.

Another benefit for generics is that they can study the commercial success of branded drugs and model the revenues available for generic versions. This provides greater assurances of profitability. Also because healthcare practitioners and patients are familiar with branded drugs before generic launch, the marketing and advertisement burdens for generics are also greatly reduced (or, simply not necessary).

Unlike branded drugs, where commercial success is predicated on discovering and securing market exclusivity for drugs addressing commercially-attractive opportunities, generic success is often dependent on successful litigation, or on maneuvering around patents and on properly estimating generic uptake and the number of other generic entrants.

Generic drug portfolio management — prioritizing which drugs to develop, and when — is challenging. There are many factors to consider, such as the manufacturing cost, the likely responses from branded drug companies, the potential for generic competition, and more.

For example, high-grossing branded drugs may attract many generic entrants, making the per-company profitability lower than for less popular drugs. Branded drug lifecycle management tactics (see the chapter on *Branded Drugs*) may also impact how many consumers switch to generics, complicating market sizing.

One way to limit competition is to aggressively pursue Paragraph IV certification opportunities. The 180-day generic exclusivity for successful patent challenge (see the chapter on *Regulatory Exclusivity*) can provide a short period of high profitability, although it may be shared with other first-filing Paragraph IV challengers and authorized generics.

Beyond simply counting the number of generic competitors it is also important to consider their size and reputation. This information can help the level of competition and also strategies for market launch and differentiation.

Many drugs may also have alternative dosage forms or new indications launched through 505(b)(2) applications. These applications can enable a generic drug to improve upon a branded drug, or to make modifications which enable them to work around process or formulation patents. A good source to identify potential 505(b)(2) entrants is clinical trials.

For example, Figure 1 shows the leading conditions being investigated for esomeprazole magnesium and indicates
that degenerative joint disease and esophageal cancer are potential brand extension opportunities. It is also important to
look for alternative salts, such as esomeprazole sodium (not
shown here) which is used in an intravenous formulation.

Figure 2 shows the leading companies conducting clinical trials with esomeprazole magnesium and indicates that
generic company Torrent Pharmaceuticals has sponsored

Clinical Trial Conditions for esomeprazole magnesium

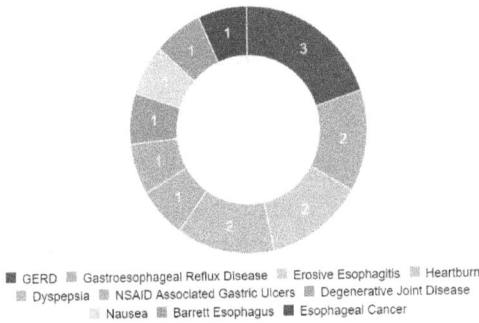

GERD ▥ Gastroesophageal Reflux Disease ▥ Erosive Esophagitis ▥ Heartburn
▥ Dyspepsia ▥ NSAID Associated Gastric Ulcers ▥ Degenerative Joint Disease
▥ Nausea ▥ Barrett Esophagus ▮ Esophageal Cancer

Figure 1: Esomeprazole magnesium clinical trial conditions investigated. *Source: DrugPatentWatch*

Clinical Trial Sponsors for esomeprazole magnesium

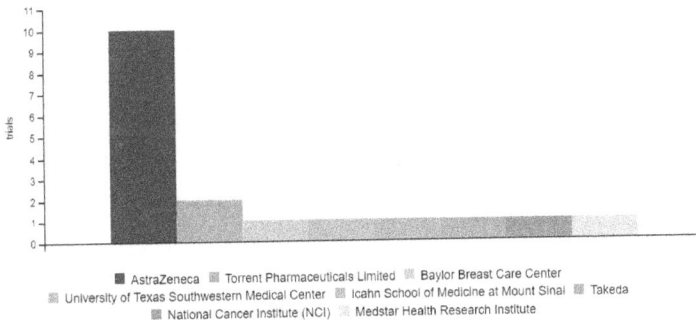

■ AstraZeneca ▥ Torrent Pharmaceuticals Limited ▥ Baylor Breast Care Center
▥ University of Texas Southwestern Medical Center ▥ Icahn School of Medicine at Mount Sinai ▥ Takeda
▥ National Cancer Institute (NCI) ▥ Medstar Health Research Institute

Figure 2: Esomeprazole magnesium clinical trial sponsors. *Source: DrugPatentWatch*

two clinical trials on the compound. A closer look at the trials can indicate potential 505(b)(2) entrants.

Other factors to investigate include revenues of branded drugs in advance of anticipated loss-of-exclusivity (see the chapter on *Market Size and Quality*). Downward trends in sales revenues or units sold may indicate that a drug is falling out of favor with prescribers; potentially due to preference for a improved derivative, or for an entirely different class of drugs.

Formulation and testing issues, as well as the projected complexity and cost of bioequivalence studies should also be considered. For example, companies with prior experience manufacturing and gaining approval for injectable drugs will find it easier and less expensive to launch an additional injectable than a company with only orally-dosed drugs in their portfolio.

Bioequivalence can also be more challenging for some categories of drugs. For example, generic substitution for branded anti-epileptic drugs has historically been problematic, as patients can be very sensitive to minor variations in bioavailability.

Table: Factors influencing generic entry decisions

	Ingredient	Recipe and testing	Capital	Distribution
Effect size	Large	Medium	Large	Medium
Reason	Suppliers centrally located and certified; compound properties known	Experience with form, family, and ingredient reduces research resource expenditure	Experience with form reduces cost to opportunity cost of a few batches rather than purchase price of one to two years	If distributing therapy already, reduces effort to find customers

Source: M. Scott Morton, Fiona. (1999). Entry Decisions in the Generic Pharmaceutical Industry. RAND Journal of Economics. 30. 421-440.

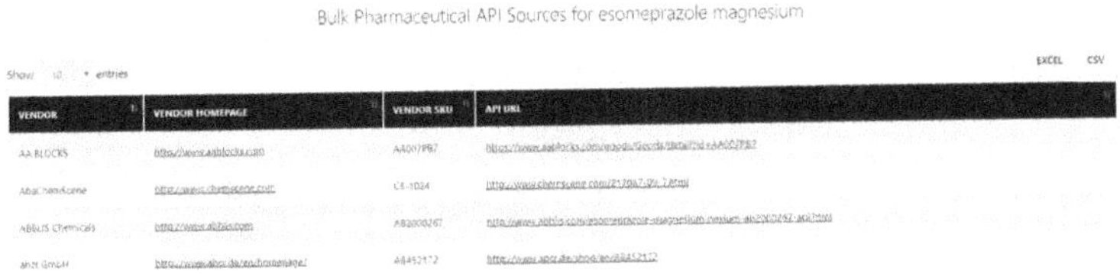

Bulk Pharmaceutical API Sources for esomeprazole magnesium

Figure 3: API suppliers for esomeprazole. *Source: DrugPatentWatch*

Once a short-list of drugs of interest is identified it is important to evaluate the quality and quantity of suppliers. If a key active pharmaceutical ingredient (API) is available from a supplier with whom a generic company has an established relationship then they can launch with greater certainty of future costs and production consistency.

An API with a small number of sources may mean that that supply-side prices will be relatively higher. Evaluation of the prices from each supplier, along with the quality and history of FDA inspections, are also important to ensure that a consistent and reliable supply of API can be ensured.

Another factor influencing generic portfolio management is synergy with existing activities. For example, if a generic company has established relationships and good reputation in distribution channels to which additional drugs can be added, then then may seek to add compatible generic drugs to their portfolio and benefit from economies of scale.

FREEDOM TO OPERATE

As described in the chapter on *Innovative and Follower Drugs*, ANDAs may not be reviewed by the FDA until one year before the NCE exclusivity expiration. Furthermore, any Paragraph IV certifications and patent lawsuits need to be resolved (or, the 30-month stay must expire) before an ANDA can be approved.

The potential for pediatric exclusivity should also be considered. Pediatric exclusivity can extend the effective period of patent protection or regulatory exclusivity by six months. If key patents do not have pediatric exclusivity applied, it is worth searching clinical trials to see if pediatric trials have been initiated. Pediatric exclusivity can also impact the NCE-1 date, making ANDA submission possible no earlier than four and half years, rather than four years, after NDA approval.

At a minimum, the status of *Orange Book* listed patents covering the API and its formulation should be clarified. Section viii carve outs may be able to work around existing patents, and Paragraph IV certifications can be used to challenge the validity of patents. If patents cannot be challenged or worked around, a paragraph III certification can ask the FDA to delay approval until patent expiration.

Beyond *Orange Book* patents it is also vital to consider both pending applications on the API or formulation, which might be listed in the *Orange Book* once they are granted, and relevant patents and pending patent applications not listed in the *Orange Book* .

Just because a drug has patents listed in the *Orange Book* does not mean that those patents prevent generic entry. While patents describing the active ingredient cannot be avoided without making a drug ineligible for an ANDA, it may be possible to design around patents directed to a formulation, composition, or polymorph while still demonstrating bioequivalence with the same active ingredient.

One way to work around formulation or API patents may be through a 505(b)(2) application which changes the protected ingredients and allows the new drug to cite the branded drug clinical trials along with bridging studies to demonstrate that the new attributes maintain safety and efficacy. Note that 505(b)(2) drugs will likely not be automatically substitutable for branded drugs. However, they if they provide therapeutic improvements on the branded drug and they may obtain preferential prescriptions. 505(b)(2) drugs are described in greater detail in the chapter on *Innovative and Follower Drugs*.

Also, because process patents, patents claiming packaging, patents claiming metabolites, and patents claiming intermediates cannot be listed in the *Orange Book* (unless they also contain claims requiring listing), it is important to ensure that such patents are identified and not infringed.

WHEN DOES LOSS-OF-EXCLUSIVITY OCCUR?

Drugs can be covered by myriad patents and regulatory protections. Even aspirin, which was first invented in 1853, still has patents (see Figure 4). For example, patent 9,226,892 describes "methods for targeted release of pharmaceuticals." Patents like this generally don't block generic entry — they cover secondary applications and improvements to drugs — but they can make the process of determining generic market entry dates complicated.

And patents are not the only ways that brands can keep generic drugs at bay. In the U.S., for example, the FDA grants temporary market exclusivity for new drugs, for new uses of existing drugs, for drugs targeting rare diseases, and more.

Finding out about loss-of-exclusivity is important to more than just generic drug companies. Healthcare payers,

US Patents and Regulatory Information for aspirin

Show 10 entries — EXCEL CSV

APPLICANT	TRADENAME	GENERIC NAME	DOSAGE	NDA	APPROVAL DATE	TE	TYPE	RLD	RS	PATENT NO.	PATENT EXPIRATION	PRODUCT	SUBSTANCE	DELIST REQ.	EXCLUSIVITY EXPIRATION
Plx Pharma	VAZALORE	aspirin	CAPSULE;ORAL	203697-001	Jan 14, 2013		OTC	Yes	Yes	9,216,150	2032-09-29	Y			
Plx Pharma	VAZALORE	aspirin	CAPSULE;ORAL	203697-001	Jan 14, 2013		OTC	Yes	Yes	9,226,892	2032-09-29				
Genus Lifesciences	YOSPRALA	aspirin; omeprazole	TABLET, DELAYED RELEASE;ORAL	205103-001	Sep 14, 2016		RX	Yes	No	9,539,214	2033-01-13				
Genus Lifesciences	YOSPRALA	aspirin; omeprazole	TABLET, DELAYED RELEASE;ORAL	205103-001	Sep 14, 2016		RX	Yes	No	9,987,231	2033-01-02				

Figure 4: Aspirin patents. *Source: DrugPatentWatch*

for example, need this information to forecast their future formulary budgets and to prepare copayment tiers to accommodate generic entry. Likewise, wholesalers and distributors need to anticipate generic availability to prevent overstock of branded drugs.

As mentioned in the chapter on *Patents and Other Forms of Intellectual Property Protection*, patents can claim different inventive steps. They may claim a drug compound, a drug's formulation, its manufacturing methods, its use for treating specific diseases, and more.

With the many patents protecting a drug it can be challenging to discern which block generic entry. The regulatory protections often expire before the patents do, but it is important to also be aware that there cases where the regulatory protections supersede the patents; so it is important to consider them as well.

Figure 5 shows the result of a freedom-to-operate analysis for Tagrisso. After examining the regulatory exclusivities, Hatch-Waxman patent extensions, and patent claims, it was determined that patent 8,946,235 was likely the dominant factor limiting generic entry. Its expiration in August 2032 (or possibly in February 2033, if the patent becomes eligible for a pediatric exclusivity extension) would create an opportunity for generic entry.

Generic Entry Opportunity Date for TAGRISSO	
Generic Entry Date for TAGRISSO*:	2032-08-08
Constraining patent/regulatory exclusivity:	8,946,235
NDA:	208065
Dosage::	TABLET;ORAL

Figure 5: Tagrisso generic drug entry date. *Source: DrugPatentWatch*

FIXED AND VARIABLE COSTS

It is important to consider fixed and variable costs separately, as well as the potential to delay, or stage, these costs. It may be possible to offset some costs until litigation outcomes, regulatory approval, or profitability become more certain. For example, approval is an up-front fixed cost and manufacturing is an ongoing variable cost.

The cost of approval may be influenced by formulation issues and by the complexity and cost of bioequivalence studies. These up-front costs will require different financing than manufacturing costs because they are essential components of an ANDA, so they will be incurred regardless of approval status. If generic entry is predicated on successful patent challenge then it may be possible to delay some costs and to also start with small-scale production until the conclusion of litigation.

Once a generic drug is on the market there may be manufacturing costs related to the ability to produce a consistently stable formulation. Unlike approval costs, these ongoing manufacturing costs may scale with production levels, and it may also be possible to factor these costs against earnings from sales. As with waiting for litigation outcomes, it may be possible to stage manufacturing investments as a hedge against smaller-than-expected commercial success.

MARKET ENTRY TIMING

The generic drug market is different from other markets because generic pharmaceutical drugs are essentially undifferentiated. They must all adhere to strict FDA standards, and hence competition is largely based on price. But the first generic drug to market can obtain a lasting advantage due to the way in which retail pharmacies and wholesalers behave.

Research from Yu Yu and Sachin Gupta at Georgia State University and Cornell University found that the first generic drug to gain market approval can enjoy an 80% market share advantage over the second entrant, and a 225% market share advantage over the third entrant. Moreover, these advantages can last for years.

One of the explanations proposed for generic first-mover advantage stems from alignment with wholesalers. Beyond considering the price of drugs, wholesalers may also make supplier decisions based on a manufacturer's reputation and history of product recalls. Likewise, retail pharmacies that buy directly from generic drug manufacturers look for availability, regularity of supplies, quick delivery, and favorable buy-back policies for unsold product.

Switching generic drug manufacturers can introduce costs of stocking and inventorying new products, and if the first-mover's product and pricing is satisfactory it can reduce the motivation to switch. So, even if lower-cost generics are available with similar reputation and other favorable characteristics, the costs of switching suppliers may allow the first entrant to maintain their contracts.

FIRST-DAY PARAGRAPH IV

First-day ANDA filers with Paragraph IV certifications may be eligible for 180 days of generic marketing exclusivity. Accordingly, many companies will elect to file their ANDA at the earliest possible date to try to obtain this exclusivity. Success is predicated on favorably litigating the patent infringement and validity issues, or on obtaining a favorable settlement with the branded company.

Other companies may prefer to wait until after the first-filer lawsuits have begun. If it is anticipated that the key patents are so sufficiently strong that first-round arguments are unlikely to succeed, then it may be better to craft second-round arguments based on observations from the first-round challengers.

Should the first-round filers succeed in invalidating the patent, companies preparing for second-round challenges can shift to a day-181 entry strategy (described below) once the 180-day generic exclusivity expires. Alternatively, these companies may seek to partner with the branded company and sell authorized generics (described in the chapter on *Innovative and Follower Drugs*).

SECOND-ROUND PARAGRAPH IV

Knowing that multiple companies are likely to file ANDAs with Paragraph IV certifications at the earliest possible opportunity, and that they may have to share the 180-day exclusivity period, some generic companies may elect to wait in the hopes that the first-round filers will fail.

While some types of patents, such as secondary patents, may be good candidates for novelty, obviousness, or other challenges, compound patents on first-in-class drugs may not have any clear weaknesses. If patent invalidation is uncertain it may be preferable to delay ANDA filing.

As described in the chapter on *Analyzing Patents and Litigation* waiting until the first-round patent challengers have failed to invalidate a patent can save costs and also enable a company to build on the failures of others. Another reason to avoid first-round ANDA filing is that if a patent challenge is successful there will likely be other first-day ANDA filers who will all share 180-day exclusivity.

Second-round Paragraph IV filers who successfully invalidate a patent may find themselves in the preferable position of having sole access to the 180-day generic exclusivity period.

LAUNCHING ON/AFTER DAY-181

While some generic companies actively pursue opportunities to challenge patents, and yet others seek opportunities to design around patents, many generic firms avoid patents entirely.

Observing the generic uptake during the 180-day exclusivity period can help second generic entrants fine-tune their launch strategies, but it also serves a greater purpose. The first generic entrants always risk infringing patents of which they were not aware, such as those not listed in the *Orange Book*. Launching on day-181 avoids this risk; if a brand had a way to keep the successful patent challenger off the market they would have used it.

So, waiting until day-181 (after the first generic patent challenger exclusivity expires) is an effective way to de-risk generic entry with minimal effort. The burden of portfolio management or pipeline prioritization is reduced, and the risk of infringing on blocking patents is also addressed.

It is also possible that patents not required to be listed in the *Orange Book* can form the basis for infringement suits. If a generic company wishes to avoid being responsible for post-launch damages it may be preferable to wait for others to launch and then re-evaluate the market opportunity.

The downside of day-181 entry is that many other generic companies are likely to also launch at the same time. This will likely result in strong price competition, impacting profitability for all players.

LITIGATE OR SETTLE

Even if a party feels that they have a strong case for (or, against) patent validity or infringement of a patent they may still prefer to settle a case rather than bear the expense of extended litigation or risk an unfavorable decision.

Reverse payment settlements, where branded firms opt to pay generic companies to delay market entry, have long been the subject of antitrust investigations. Accordingly, these terms of agreements have evolved and become increasingly complex to avoid antitrust issues.

Branded companies have trended towards partnering on generic entry, rather than simply paying generic companies not to launch. These agreements can provide branded drug companies an opportunity to reduce litigation expenses and avoid the potential for adverse court decisions, while positioning a generic company to reap the enduring benefits of first-entry.

It may also be possible (and profitable) to sell an ANDA. Because only the first-day filers are eligible for 180-day market exclusivity, it may make sense for a first-day filer to sell an ANDA to a company with more experience in winning patent challenges.

For non-*Orange Book* patents it may be preferable to file an *inter partes* review (IPR) before the Patent Trial and Appeal Board (PTAB). ANDA filers with Paragraph IV certification against *Orange Book* patents may be able to benefit from 180-day marketing exclusivity; for non-*Orange Book* patents this opportunity does not exist, which may favor IPR.

IPRs can also be used tactically if a generic company is not among the group with first-day ANDA Paragraph IV certifications. Using an IPR to invalidate a patent may start the 75-day clock for generic launch. Should the IPR successfully invalidate a patent and the ANDA first-day filers fail to launch within that window they may lose their 180-day marketing exclusivity.

SKINNY LABEL / OFF-LABEL USE

As described earlier it may be possible for generics to use a Section viii carve out statement (also called a skinny label) to work around patents. As described in the section on *Patent Claims* in the chapter on *Analyzing Patents and Litigation*, the protected aspects of a drug can include the active compound, the formulation, and individual uses.

If the compound and formulation are are unpatented or if their patents have expired, *and* if there are multiple approved therapeutic indications, then there may be an opportunity to *carve out* patented indications and gain generic approval for the unpatented indications.

For example, if there are no active patents covering a drug's active ingredient or formulation, and its label mentions indications A and B, then so long as either indication A or B does not have patent protection a generic company can file a Section viii statement to seek ANDA approval for only the unpatented indication.

An important consideration when using a carve out is that the FDA prohibits drug companies from promoting unapproved uses, and patent law prohibits inducement of patent infringement. If successful generic entry is predicated on prescription for the patented indication (e.g. the patented indication is the commercial target), then success may depend on physicians independently prescribing the generic *off-label* for the patented indication.

FINDING LOW-COMPETITION OPPORTUNITIES

Beyond aggressively pursuing emerging opportunities such as NCE-1 dates and patent expirations, it is also viable to find opportunities in drugs with little competition. As mentioned in the chapter on *Regulatory Exclusivity*, the FDA has special incentives for generic entry into markets for which there is inadequate competition.

DISCONTINUED DRUGS

Not all drugs are withdrawn from the market due to safety issues or lack of efficacy. Some may simply cost too much to manufacture, or they may fall below the revenue threshold of a large company.

For a small generic company, successful drugs abandoned by larger players may represent attractive market opportunities. These drugs can also help establish new channels, or they can leverage existing relationships in preferred markets.

For drugs which were discontinued because of manufacturing costs it is worth studying expired patents and other advances in manufacturing technologies, such as switching from continuous to batch manufacturing. Reducing manufacturing costs can increase the profitability of a drug, enabling it to be sold at lower prices and possibly earning a larger market-share than previously realized.

DRUGS WITH NO PATENTS AND NO COMPETITION

Just as drugs may be discontinued for economic reasons, there are also dozens of drugs with no patent or regulatory

Off-Patent Drugs With No Active Sources (Discontinued Drugs)

Figure 6: Discontinued drugs. *Source: DrugPatentWatch*

Off-Patent Drugs With 1 Source

Glossary

Show 10 ▾ entries

EXCEL   CSV

APPLICANT	TRADENAME	GENERIC NAME	DOSAGE	NDA	APPROVAL DATE	TE	TYPE	RLD	RS	STRENGTH
Abbvie	SURVANTA	beractant	SUSPENSION;INTRATRACHEAL	020032-001	Jul 1, 1991		RX	Yes	Yes	25MG/ML
Abbvie	TRIDIONE	trimethadione	TABLET;ORAL	005856-008	Approved Prior to Jan 1, 1982		RX	Yes	Yes	150MG
Academic Pharma Inc	BRETYLIUM TOSYLATE	bretylium tosylate	INJECTABLE;INJECTION	204866-001	Dec 21, 2018		RX	No	Yes	50MG/ML

Figure 7: Single-source drugs. *Source: DrugPatentWatch*

exclusivity and only one source.

There are several reasons why a drug may have no protection and no competitors. For drugs with small markets there may simply be not many companies interested in selling it. The sole manufacturer could be a small firm that is satisfied with the small market, or it could be a large firm that continues to sell a drug years after developing it. Some of these drugs may represent opportunities for market expansion through better product market positioning, reformulation, or finding new indications.

UNAPPROVED DRUGS: OPPORTUNITIES FOR RAPID APPROVAL AND MARKET EXCLUSIVITY

Contrary to popular belief, there are many unapproved drugs which are actively being used (see Figure 8). Many physicians may not even realize that that the drugs they are prescribing have not had thorough tests for safety and efficacy. The reason why these drugs are on the market relates to the history of FDA regulations, and the FDA is actively trying to encourage the development of approvable versions of these unapproved drugs.

The FDA currently requires that any new drug must be proven to be both safe and effective prior to receiving marketing authorization, but this was not always the case. In

Unapproved (DESI) Drugs

DRUG NAME	GENERIC NAME	TYPE	DOSAGE	ROUTE	MARKETING START	MARKETING END	SUPPLIER
Aloquin	Iodoquinol and aloe vera leaf	HUMAN PRESCRIPTION DRUG	GEL	TOPICAL	2015-03-01		Novum Pharma LLC
Alpha-Pro	Sodium Fluoride and Hydrofluoric Acid	HUMAN PRESCRIPTION DRUG	GEL	DENTAL	2011-04-01		Dentsa Technologies Inc
ALTACAINE	Tetracaine Hydrochloride	HUMAN PRESCRIPTION DRUG	SOLUTION	OPHTHALMIC	2002-02-01		Altaire Pharmaceuticals Inc
ALTAFLUOR	Fluorescein Sodium and Benoxinate Hydrochloride	HUMAN PRESCRIPTION DRUG	SOLUTION	OPHTHALMIC	2000-06-21		Altaire Pharmaceuticals Inc

Figure 8: Unapproved (DESI) drugs. *Source: DrugPatentWatch*

1938 the Federal Food Drug and Cosmetics Act required that drugs be proven safe before coming to the market.

In 1962, Congress amended the 1938 law to require manufacturers to show that their drug products were effective, as well as safe. As a result, all drugs approved between 1938 and 1962 had to be reviewed again for effectiveness. The FDA launched the Drug Efficacy Study Implementation, or DESI, program to classify the these drugs as 'effective', 'ineffective', or 'needing further study' and effective drugs were permitted to remain on the market.

The FDA has stated its intention to initiate enforcement action against unapproved drugs, providing an incentive for companies seeking approval while simultaneously removing unapproved drugs from the market.

In seeking approval for unapproved drugs it may be possible to cite information from their prior use, saving development costs and making them eligible for a 505(b)(2) approval pathway. If clinical studies are required a drug may obtain 3 years of regulatory exclusivity, and it it contains a never-before approved chemical entity it may be eligible for 5 years of regulatory exclusivity.

GENERICS OUTSIDE THE U.S.

The lack of price controls in the U.S., combined with regulations to encourage generic entry, result in high rates of generic entry. Countries with a smaller addressable market, for example, may result in less competition because fewer generic companies seek approval. Further, price controls on branded drugs may mean that generic substitution does not present the cost-savings seen in the U.S. Likewise, in other countries generic drugs may face price controls, limiting the appeal for generic producers. Figure 5 in the chapter on *Innovative and Branded Drugs* shows generic adoption rates between countries.

GENERIC ENTRY IN EUROPE

In Europe, generic drugs account for around half the market by volume, which is much less than the roughly 90% volume seen in the U.S. There are many explanations for this difference, including reduced incentive for generic entry due to price controls on branded drugs and the fragmentation of the individual-country markets in Europe.

Pricing and reimbursement policies in Europe are complicated. Each country has its own set of policies governing generics. The result has been uneven penetration of generics in different European countries.

Germany currently has the greatest generic drug penetration, followed by Poland and the UK, and then Russia. This still leaves plenty of European countries where generic drug penetration is lower, and where opportunities for generic drug market entry can be promising.

According to consulting firm Deloitte, a single approach to generic drug entry across Europe is unlikely to succeed. There is too much variation among European countries in terms of how generics are prescribed, dispensed, and purchased, for a single approach to work everywhere.

Prescriptions are written either using the International Non-Proprietary Name (INN) or the specific generic brand name, and different countries tend toward one or the other. In the INN-prescribing countries, price is the primary strategic driver. In countries that prescribe using specific generic brand name, strong customer service and a local sales force are strategic drivers.

In individual European markets, drugs may be primarily dispensed at independent pharmacies or in larger chains. When chains dominate, wholesaler and distributor availability become more important. When independent pharmacies dominate, a strong distribution network and sales force become more important.

European markets may or may not purchase drugs through a tendering process. Tendering is a cost-control mechanism designed for lowering unit prices, and has become more popular among large European payers and hospitals. In markets where the tendering process is used, margins are typically smaller, but market entry can be faster, benefiting generic makers with low production costs.

In Germany INN prescribing is favored, and dispensing of drugs is influenced by the country's insurance fund. Drugs are purchased using a tendering system. Therefore, generic manufacturers with low production costs, broad portfolios, and stable supplies would be likeliest to succeed there.

In Russia, INN prescribing is required, and drugs are primarily dispensed through chain pharmacies. Drugs are purchased both through a tendering system and through the private market. Consequently, generic manufacturers with strong product brand recognition, with local sales forces, and with extensive regulatory and political experience would be likelier to succeed.

BRANDED GENERICS

Branded generics are generic drugs that have been given a proprietary market name. They may be marketed similarly to branded innovative drugs. Unlike branded drugs, which are approved under NDAs and generic drugs, are approved under ANDAs, branded drugs may be approved by either route.

In emerging markets where consumers and pharmacies may want additional assurances of the quality and purity of their drugs, well-known multinational firms may brand their generic drugs.

Ordinary generic drugs are usually known simply by their chemical name. For example, generic versions of the branded drug Lipitor are sold as atorvastatin calcium.

Branded generics, however, are given names to drive recognition and promote consumer loyalty. For example, Cryselle is a branded generic contraceptive pill which was approved through an ANDA. It goes by Cryselle rather than its generic name (norgestrel and ethinyl estradiol) to increase the likelihood of patients requesting it by name.

Table: Branded, authorized, and *traditional* generics

	Branded Generic	Authorized Generic	Traditional Generic
FDA Approval Process	ANDA or 505(b)(2)	NDA	ANDA
Relation to Patent Expiration	Sold after branded drug patent expiration	Can be sold before drug patent expiration	Sold after branded drug patent expiration
Cost	Typically more than unbranded generic, less than branded drug	Typically more than unbranded generic, less than branded drug	Typically cheaper than branded or authorized generics

Some branded generics are derivatives of off-patent drugs. These drugs are generally approved through a 505(b)(2) application rather than an ANDA, so they are given a unique name to help differentiate them from other generic drugs. For example Abraxane is a branded form of paclitaxel which was originally approved under the brand name Taxol. Abraxane improves on the original paclitaxel by formulating it as albumin-bound nanoparticles. This modification, which necessitated a 505(b)(2) approval, results in reduced toxicity, longer-acting doses, and improved patient compliance.

Another reason to launch branded generics is to leverage well-respected commercial brands. In the U.S. branded generics have a very limited share of the market. By contrast, in India and China they command more than 50% of revenues. The rationale for this stronger representation is twofold. Firstly, generic substitution laws in the U.S. limit market domination of any single generic. Secondly, branded generics leverage the trust that prescribers, patients, and pharmacists may have for multinational brands.

For example, Abbott spun-off a new company called Abbvie with a focus on novel drugs, while the legacy Abbott would retain medical device, diagnostic, and branded generics businesses. One of Abbott's branded generic products,

Figure 9: Abbott's Duphabears *Source: Abbott*

Duphabears is shown in Figure 9. Duphabears is a fruit-flavored gummy bear containing a laxative for children, only available in emerging markets.

In terms of price, both branded generics and authorized generics tend to cost more than ordinary generics, but less than branded drugs with unexpired drug patents. The following table shows some of the main differences among branded generics, authorized generics, and ordinary generics.

Case Study: Identifying First Generic Entrants

When patents and regulatory protections expire, the market for generic entry is open. But, generics can enter prior to anticipated patent expiration dates if they can work around patents or invalidate them.

Although the Food and Drug Administration (FDA) does not provide information on the identities of companies that file generic drug applications, there are ways to proactively identify generic entrants before they launch. This information is important for many parties. For examples, payers need to know who the first generic entrants will be to adjust their co-payment tiers, to establish substitution rules in advance of generic entry, and to ensure that their budgetary estimates are aligned with market conditions. Likewise, wholesalers and distributors can use knowledge of impending generic entry to avoid overstock of branded drugs and to establish contracts for generic drugs.

Branded and generic firms need to be aware of generic entrants so they can make informed decisions based on historic knowledge of drug pricing strategies, market entry approaches, and opportunities for competition.

Paragraph IV (Patent) Challenges for VIMPAT				
DRUGNAME	DOSAGE	STRENGTH	RLD	DATE
lacosamide	Injection	10 mg/mL, 20 mL	Vimpat	2016-06-30
lacosamide	Tablets	50 mg, 100 mg, 150 mg, and 200 mg	Vimpat	2012-10-29
lacosamide	Oral Solution	10 mg/mL	Vimpat	2012-10-29

Figure 1: Paragraph IV certifications for Vimpat. *Source: DrugPatentWatch*

STARTING WITH PATENT CHALLENGES

Patent challenges are an important part of tracking generic entry. If a generic drug company can successfully invalidate a patent or prove that their drug doesn't infringe on branded drug patents, then they can launch well before patent expiration dates.

In the U.S. patent challenges are formalized through the Paragraph IV certification process (see Figure 1). Tracking Paragraph IV challenges is a quick and effective way to anticipate generic entry in advance of patent expiration dates.

A limitation of tracking Paragraph IV certifications is that while they can help anticipate early generic entry opportunities, they do not name the potential first generic entrant.

Because the FDA does not disclose the names of companies filing Paragraph IV certifications, nor the contents of drug applications, it is not possible to directly ascertain the name of the Paragraph IV patent challenger.

TENTATIVE APPROVALS

Tentative approvals are clearances for drugs to be marketed, but for the existence of patents or market exclusivities. According to the FDA:

If a generic drug product is ready
for approval before the expiration of
any patents or exclusivities accorded
to the reference listed drug product, FDA issues a tentative approval
letter to the applicant. The tentative
approval letter details the circum-
stances associated with the tentative
approval. FDA delays final approval
of the generic drug product until all
patent or exclusivity issues have been
resolved. A tentative approval does
not allow the applicant to market the
generic drug product.

Because successful Paragraph IV challengers often want
to launch as soon as possible following a successful outcome
(and, potentially to demonstrate confidence in the strength
of their case), they will often obtain tentative approvals for
the drugs for which they have launched patent challenges.

So, looking at the recent tentative approvals (see Figure 2)
can provide an indication of who the Paragraph IV filer may be.

Generic filers with tentative approvals for LACOSAMIDE

Applicant	Application No.	Strength	Dosage Form
Glenmark Pharms Ltd	204980	10MG/ML	SOLUTION;ORAL
Glenmark Pharms Ltd	205006	150MG	TABLET;ORAL

Figure 2: Tentative approvals for lacosamide. *Source: DrugPatentWatch*

Note: an added feature of tentative approvals is that drugs being distributed under the President's Emergency Plan for AIDS Relief (PEPFAR) must either have traditional FDA approval, or a tentative approval. Therefore tentative approvals can, even in the absence of impending patent expiration or invalidation, provide market entry opportunities.

PATENT LITIGATION

There are two methods of challenging patents in the U.S. Regardless of the method used to challenge a patent, the parties involved will be named and the proceedings will be made public, so examining the litigants can identify the Paragraph IV filer, and therefore the first potential generic entrant.

The older, and more comprehensive, method is conventional litigation in district courts (see Figure 3). Generic companies must send branded companies a notice of their Paragraph IV certification within 20 days of confirmation of ANDA receipt by the FDA. Branded firms have 45 from receipt of the notice letter to file a patent infringement lawsuit and gain an automatic 30-month stay on ANDA approval.

District court litigation is where branded company infringement cases will be raised, so looking at the defendants in these cases can identify Paragraph IV filers.

Generic companies can also launch patent validity challenges before the Patent Trial and Appeal Board (See Figure 4). These challenges are not eligible for 180-day generic market exclusivity so they are not frequently used by Paragraph

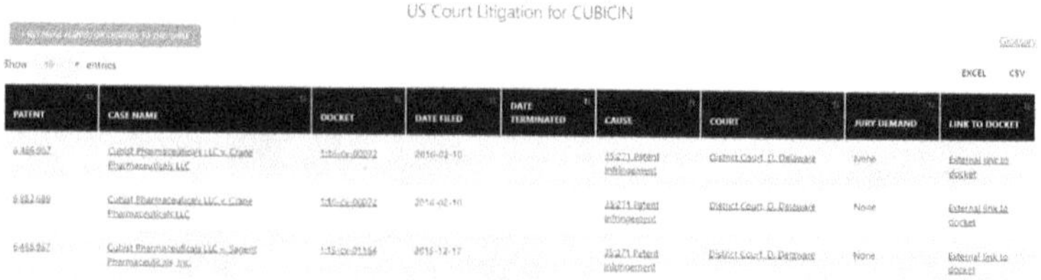
US Court Litigation for CUBICIN

Show 10 entries

EXCEL CSV

PATENT	CASE NAME	DOCKET	DATE FILED	DATE TERMINATED	CAUSE	COURT	JURY DEMAND	LINK TO DOCKET
6,468,967	Cubist Pharmaceuticals LLC v. Crane Pharmaceuticals LLC	1:16-cv-00072	2016-02-10		35:271 Patent Infringement	District Court, D. Delaware	None	External link to docket
6,852,689	Cubist Pharmaceuticals LLC v. Crane Pharmaceuticals LLC	1:16-cv-00072	2016-02-10		35:271 Patent Infringement	District Court, D. Delaware	None	External link to docket
6,468,967	Cubist Pharmaceuticals LLC v. Sagent Pharmaceuticals, Inc.	1:15-cv-01164	2015-12-17		35:271 Patent Infringement	District Court, D. Delaware	None	External link to docket

Figure 3: Cubicin patent infringement litigation. *Source: DrugPatentWatch*

Patent Trial and Appeal Board Cases for ACZONE

Glossary

Show 10 entries

EXCEL CSV

PATENT	PETITIONER	STATUS	FILING DATE	ACCORDED FILING DATE	PATENT OWNER	TRIAL TYPE	TRIAL NUMBER	DECISION DATE	INVENTOR	DOCUMENT DOWNLOAD
9,517,219	Mylan Pharmaceuticals Inc.	Notice Of Filing Date Accorded	2019-06-07	2019-06-07	Warner et al	Inter partes review	IPR2019-01095			Download case documents from USPTO
9,517,219	Amneal Pharmaceuticals LLC	Instituted	2018-11-06	2018-11-06	Warner et al	Inter partes review	IPR2019-00207	2019-05-10		Download case documents from USPTO

Figure 4: PTAB cases for Aczone. *Source: DrugPatentWatch*

IV filers, but they can be effective sources of identifying potential generic entrants not using the Paragraph IV certification pathway.

PRESS RELEASES AND PUBLIC DISCLOSURES

Another approach is to examine press releases mentioning the drug for which a patent challenge has been filed.

Publicly-traded companies are required to promptly publicly disclose many types of information, and this means that challengers and defendants in patent invalidity suits will often be compelled to disclose the existence of patent litigation, along with the names of the parties involved. So even if only one party is publicly-traded, their disclosures can still name the other party.

Figure 5 shows a filing from BioDelivery Sciences disclosing that Actavis had filed an ANDA with a Paragraph IV certification. Note that they refer to receipt of a *purported* notice; successfully disputing the validity of a notice letter can derail a Paragraph IV certification.

Additionally, even private companies (not subject to the same disclosure requirements as publicly-traded companies) have an incentive to announce Paragraph IV certifications. Issuing press releases announcing their patent challenges can help establish distribution and supply-chain relationships in anticipation of generic launch.

Item 8.01Other Events

On February 8, 2016, BioDelivery Sciences International, Inc. (the "Company") received a purported notice relating to a paragraph IV certification from Actavis Laboratories UT, Inc. ("Actavis") seeking to find invalid three Orange Book listed patents of the Company (the "Patents") relating specifically to the Company's BUNAVAIL® buccal film for the maintenance treatment of opioid dependence. The paragraph IV certification relates to an Abbreviated New Drug Application (the "ANDA") filed by Actavis with the U.S Food and Drug Administration ("FDA") for a generic formulation of BUNAVAIL. The Patents subject to Acatvis' certification (which relate to the Company's BEMA® film delivery technology) are U.S. Patent Nos. 7,579,019 ("the '019 Patent"), 8,147,866 and 8,703,177.

The Company believes that Actavis' claims of invalidity of the Patents are wholly without merit and, as it has done in the past, the Company intends to vigorously defend its intellectual property. The Company is highly confident that the Patents are valid, as evidenced in part by the

Figure 5: Company filing disclosure identifies Paragraph IV filer. *Source: U.S. Securities and Exchange Commission*

Case Study: Viagra Generic Entry

The story of Viagra's patents and the generic entry of sildenafil citrate is a valuable one because it covers many of the nuances of drug patenting and generic entry in the U.S.

Pfizer used multiple patents, a Hatch-Waxman patent term extension, a pediatric extension, litigation, an out-of-court settlement, and an authorized generic fighter brand to protect the market for Viagra.

Viagra was approved in 1998, and the original patent covering Viagra was 5,250,534. This patent received a 283-day Hatch-Waxman patent term extension giving it an expiration date of March 29th, 2012. This 14-year patent life is longer than for many other drugs, but Pfizer was able extend the patent-protected life even further.

Patent 5,250,534 was filed in 1990, and in 1994 (four years prior to Viagra's launch) Pfizer filed a second patent: 6,469,012. Because patent 6,469,012 was filed prior to June 8th 1995, its term is *17 years from the grant date*, rather than *20 years from the filing date*, which is how expiration is determined for patents filed after Jun 8th 1995.

Patent 6,469,012 was granted on October 22nd, 2002, so the original expiration date was set to October 22nd, 2019 — more than twenty years after the drug's launch. The patent's expiration was extended to April 22nd, 2020 because Pfizer responded to an FDA request to perform pediatric clinical trials, granting six months of pediatric exclusivity protection.

PATENT CHALLENGES AND OUT OF COURT SETTLEMENT

Pfizer successfully defended Viagra's patents in many patent litigations, but one lawsuit stands out. Despite prevailing in a lawsuit against Teva which affirmed the validity of patent 6,469,012, in 2013 Pfizer announced an out-of-court settlement with Teva. This agreement granted Teva a license to manufacture and sell generic sildenafil citrate starting in December 2017, more than two years before Viagra's patent expiration. Importantly, this was not a "reverse-payment" patent settlement, as rather than simply delaying their launch in exchange for payment Teva was required to pay Pfizer a licensing fee to produce the generic.

LAUNCHING AN AUTHORIZED GENERIC TO FIGHT GENERIC ENTRY

Generic drugs sell at a discount to the branded version, which hurts branded revenues, but there are things which brands can do to limit the impact.

A popular tactic is to launch an authorized generic. In this strategy a branded firm licenses a third party to market the branded drug under another name, compelling the generic entrant (in this case Teva) to compete in the generic market. The authorized generic for Viagra was Revatio and it was licensed to several suppliers (see Figure 1).

REVATIO

Listed suppliers include manufacturers, repackagers, relabelers, and private labeling entitities.

Show 10 entries   EXCEL   CSV

APPLICANT	TRADENAME	GENERIC NAME	DOSAGE	NDA	NDA/ANDA	SUPPLIER	PACKAGE CODE	PACKAGE
Pfizer	REVATIO	sildenafil citrate	TABLET;ORAL	021845	NDA AUTHORIZED GENERIC	Greenstone LLC	59762-0083-1	90 TABLET, FILM COATED in 1 BOTTLE (59762-0083-1)
Pfizer	REVATIO	sildenafil citrate	TABLET;ORAL	021845	NDA AUTHORIZED GENERIC	Aphena Pharma Solutions - Tennessee, LLC	43353-345-53	60 TABLET, FILM COATED in 1 BOTTLE (43353-345-53)
Pfizer	REVATIO	sildenafil citrate	TABLET;ORAL	021845	NDA AUTHORIZED GENERIC	Aphena Pharma Solutions - Tennessee, LLC	43353-345-20	20 TABLET, FILM COATED in 1 BOTTLE (43353-345-20)

Figure 1: Revatio suppliers. *Source: DrugPatentWatch*

LESSONS FOR PREDICTING GENERIC ENTRY

The story of Viagra and the generic entry of sildenafil citrate illustrates the value of patent and litigation data and the need to continuously re-evaluate factors affecting generic entry. Reliance on the first patent would have vastly underestimated the date of generic entry, and looking solely at the expiration date of the second patent would have missed the December 2017 generic entry.

Case Study: Extracting Competitive Intelligence From Litigation

Many kinds of competitive and business intelligence can be obtained by studying litigation.

For example, a company seeking to license a drug to, or from, another party may want to know what terms the other party has agreed to in other instances. The specific terms of agreements between companies are generally not disclosed, but they may become available should a court case necessitate their mention.

When facing patent litigation it can be very useful to know how aggressive the other party is, and also what settlement terms they may accept.

When parties agree to a out-of-court settlement *in lieu* of continuing with litigation the terms of the settlement are generally not publicly disclosed. But, subsequent lawsuits can reveal the terms of a settlement. This knowledge can be used in future litigation to predict what terms a party may find acceptable in an out-of-court settlement.

The case of *Teikoku Pharma USA, Inc. v. Endo Pharmaceuticals, Inc.* illustrates how information about an out-of-court settlement can be revealed in subsequent litigation. In this case Teikoku asserted that they had an agreement with

Endo in which Endo would reimburse Teikoku for expenses incurred in pursuing patent infringement claims against third parties, and that Endo had failed to satisfy the terms of that agreement (see Figure 1).

If true, the *Nature of the Action* reveals firstly that future partners may want to consider asking for Endo to cover litigation expenses. For it appears that Endo is willing to accommodate these terms in their partnership agreements.

It is also worth noting that partners with Endo who have expense-recovery clauses in their agreements should review the full proceedings of the litigation to ascertain the merits of the complaint and gauge the likelihood of receiving compensation for pursuing patent infringers.

HOW MUCH WILL A COMPANY SPEND TO PURSUE PATENT INFRINGERS?

The risk of being sued for patent infringement is a persistent concern among generic companies. Even in cases where generic firms are confident that they are not infringing any patents there remains the risk that a patent holder will view the situation differently and pursue legal action.

So, an important consideration in launching generic drugs is to evaluate the strength of cases which may be brought by patent owners, and the resources which the patent owners may dedicate to challenging infringers.

Figure 2 provides key insights into Teikoku's tactics in

NATURE OF THE ACTION

4.   This is an action for breach of contract. Endo agreed to use any recovery from a settlement to reimburse Teikoku for out-of-pocket costs and expenses (including attorneys' fees) incurred in pursuing patent infringement claims against third parties. Despite receiving a generous recovery through just such a settlement, Endo now refuses to reimburse Teikoku's out-of-pocket expenses.

Figure 1: Teikoku sues Endo for patent litigation expenses. *Source: U.S. Courts*

21.   On May 28, 2012, after post-trial briefing, but before the trial court had issued a decision on the merits, the parties entered into a Settlement and License Agreement (the "Settlement Agreement").

22.   As of that date, Teikoku incurred in the Watson Litigation unreimbursed out-of-pocket costs and expenses (including attorneys' fees) of $2,313,496.99.

23.   Through the Settlement Agreement, Endo and Teikoku agreed to release the claims they had asserted against Watson in the Watson Litigation and to other consideration. In return, among other things, Watson agreed to pay Endo a royalty equal to 25% of all gross profits enjoyed by Watson from the sale of generic Lidoderm® for a defined period of time. At the time the parties executed the Settlement Agreement, it was uncertain whether Watson would ever make any royalty payments to Endo as Watson's proposed generic product had not, at that time, been approved by the FDA.

Figure 2: Legal expenses and settlement terms. *Source: U.S. Courts*

pursuing perceived patent infringers. Firstly, they spent $2.3 million in litigation against Watson, and secondly they entered into a settlement agreement to resolve the dispute. A deeper look into Teikoku's litigation with Watson could yield additional insights into the other tactics employed by Teikoku.

As demonstrated in this case, companies being challenged by Teikoku for patent infringement may anticipate that Teikoku will spend at least $2.3 million on their prosecution of the case. Further, should a defendant elect to offer a settlement they may believe that Teikoku will accept a royalty of 25% of gross profits. Conversely, plaintiffs asserting patents against Watson may expect that Watson will agree to pay a 25% royalty to resolve the litigation.

HOW MUCH WAS EARNED IN ROYALTIES?

In addition to extracting the terms of Teikoku's partnership terms with Endo, and further learning about Teikoku's tactics in pursuing perceived infringers, it is still possible to learn more from this case.

25.   From September 15, 2013 to the present, Endo received royalty payments from Watson of over $100 million, an amount substantially exceeding the combined expenses incurred by Endo and Teikoku in bringing the Watson Litigation. These royalty payments constitute a "recovery obtained as a result of the Suit" as that term in used in the Letter Agreement.

26.   Although Teikoku has demanded reimbursement of the expenses it incurred in bringing the suit, Endo has refused to so reimburse Teikoku.

Figure 3: Royalty payments received. *Source: U.S. Courts*

Teikoku's assertions in Figure 3 claim that Endo earned over $100mm in license fees from Watson over the roughly 21 month timespan cited. Back-calculating from the 25% royalty rate over nearly two years, it would appear that Watson's sales were over $200mm/year.

Beyond learning about Endo's royalty earnings or Watson's revenues from generic drug sales, tactical information can also be gleaned from this case. For example, generic companies often have base parameters which define which opportunities they will pursue. From this case it would appear that Watson finds a $200mm/year revenue projection attractive when deciding to develop a generic drug.

Appendices

DRUG NAMES

The following excerpt, reprinted with permission from *Building Biotechnology*, describes the various names attributed to drugs, and the utility of each name. For a comprehensive list of generic name stems see https://www.drugpatentwatch.com/blog/a-comprehensive-generic-drug-naming-resource

Drugs have several types of names, each of which is used for a different context. Chemical and biological names are respectively used to describe the composition of small-molecule or biological drugs. Generic names are shared between branded and generic drugs to indicate common ingredients.

Table 1: Types of drug names

Chemical / Biological	Scientific description of drug compound
Generic	Simplified name based on drug function
Trade Name	Branded name, protected by trademark law

Table 2: Selected generic drug naming conventions

Name Element	Category	Examples
-vit	antivirals	acyclovir, combivir
-mab	monoclonal antibodies	cetuximab (ImClone's Erbitux), rituximab (Biogen Idec's Rituxan)
-rsen	antisense oligonucleotides	fomivirsen (Isis Pharmaceutical's Vitravene)

The trade name of a drug is the proprietary name used by different firms to brand their products.

The chemical or biological name of a drug is determined using several conventions, the objectives of which are to provide scientific descriptions of the composition of a drug. The chemical name for ibuprofen, for example, is 2-[4-(2-methylpropyl) phenyl]propanoic acid; the biological name for Amgen's Epogen is recombinant erythropoietin. The generic name of a drug is created using a specific nomenclature system and is used to identify generic versions of a branded drug. The generic name for Amgen's Epogen is epoetin alfa. Ibuprofen is the generic name for a drug which has been marketed under Advil (Wyeth), Motrin (Mc-Neil), and other trade names.

Trade names are used to uniquely brand an individual company's version of a drug. A drug's proprietary or trade name must be approved by the FDA and cannot imply efficacy. Trade names are protected by trademark law, preventing generic companies from using them even after patents expire, and encouraging pioneers to develop strong brand identity to extend their market dominance past patent expiration. Despite the restriction that trade names cannot imply efficacy, drug makers often select names with connotations aligned with a drug's intended use. Vick's Dayquil and Nyquil respectively suggest daytime or night time tranquility in treating cold and flu symptoms.

Other useful names such as abbreviations (EPO is a common substitute for epoetin alfa) may be used when appropriate. Drugs in development are referred to by their method of action (e.g., ACE inhibitor) or internal code name (e.g., MEDI-493 was an internal code name for MedImmune's Synagis).

Reprinted with permission from Building Biotechnology

FDA ORANGE BOOK

The U.S. Food and Drug Administration (FDA) publishes a list of approved drugs and patents, named *Approved Drug Products with Therapeutic Equivalence Evaluations*. Because the original print version had an orange cover, it is more commonly known as the *Orange Book*.

The *Orange Book* originated in 1980 and is published in annual editions with monthly supplements. The primary objective of the *Orange Book* is to serve as an authoritative source of which drugs have been approved by the FDA, and which drugs can be safely substituted for each other. This imperative emerged from a desire to provide a single central list based on common criteria which would be preferable to evaluating drug products on the basis of differing definitions and criteria previously implemented by various state laws.

The Federal government, wishing to promote interchangeability and drive commerce, spurred the FDA to create a list of approved drugs and therapeutic equivalence determinations. The current *Orange Book* is accessible online at https://www.fda.gov/media/71474/

Archives dating back to the first edition (1980) are available at https://www.drugpatentwatch.com/orange-book.php

THERAPEUTIC EQUIVALENCE (TE)

For generic drugs to help drive down drug prices after patent expiration it is essential that they be reliable substitutes for branded drugs. Patients and physicians need assurances that a generic drug will produce the same clinical effect and have the same safety profile as the prescribed product. The purpose of the FDA's therapeutic equivalence ratings is to provide these assurances.

Branded and generic drugs are considered to be therapeutically equivalent only if they contain the same active ingredient(s), share common dosage forms and routes of administration, and have the same strength.

The first letter of the TE code indicates the level of therapeutic equivalence. Drugs for which the generic application satisfactorily demonstrates therapeutic equivalence are A-rated, and drugs which the FDA does not deem to be therapeutically equivalent are B-rated.

Because "A"-rated drugs are considered to be equivalent to each other, pharmacists can substitute A-rated generics for branded drugs where permitted or legally required.

Both A- and B-ratings are refined into subcategories. For example, an AA-rating indicates that ingredients and dosage forms present neither actual or potential bioequivalence problems. Some dosage forms are assigned specific codes based on criteria used to demonstrate bioequivalence. For example AN is used for for aerosolized drugs, AO for injectable oil solutions, AP for injectable aqueous solutions, and AT for topical products.

AB ratings indicate that actual or potential bioequivalence problems have been resolved through adequate in vivo and/or in vitro testing. In some cases an additional digit is added to the rating to refine the substitutability.

For example there may be multiple drug variants which all contain the same ingredient, with the same strength and

B-Rated Generic Drugs with no A-rated Versions

Show 10 entries

EXCEL CSV

APPLICANT	TRADENAME	GENERIC NAME	DOSAGE	NDA	APPROVAL DATE	TE	TYPE	RLD	RS	PATENT NO.	PATENT EXPIRATION	PRODUCT	SUBSTANCE	DELIST REQ.	EXCLUSIVITY EXPIRATION
Actavis Elizabeth	PROPYLTHIOURACIL	propylthiouracil	TABLET;ORAL	080172-001	Approved Prior to Jan 1, 1982	BD	RX	No	No						
Alembic Pharms Ltd	DESVENLAFAXINE	desvenlafaxine	TABLET, EXTENDED RELEASE;ORAL	204150-001	Mar 4, 2013	BC	RX	Yes	Yes						
Alembic Pharms Ltd	DESVENLAFAXINE	desvenlafaxine	TABLET, EXTENDED RELEASE;ORAL	204150-002	Mar 4, 2013	BC	RX	Yes	Yes						

Figure 1: Non-bioequivalent generic drugs. *Source: DrugPatentWatch*

dosage form, yet they are not bioequivalent to each other. In these instances, there will be more than one reference listed drug (RLD), and any generic seeking approval must prove bioequivalence to one particular RLD. In order to avoid confusion, the FDA assigns numbers to TE codes to differentiate which RLD a generic is equivalent to. For example, a generic rated AB1 can be substituted for a brand rated AB1, but can not be substituted for a brand rated AB2.

B-rated Drugs are those which the FDA considers not to be therapeutically equivalent due to actual or potential bioequivalence problems which have not been resolved. B-rated drugs are generally not legally substitutable.

As with A-rated drugs, there are subcategories for B-rated drugs. A BC-rating indicates extended-release dosage forms which are formulated to make a drug available over an extended period of time. A BD-rating indicates active ingredients and dosage forms with documented bioequivalence problems. BE ratings are used to reference delayed-release oral dosage forms.

FREE PATENT DATABASES

European Patent Office
https://www.epo.org/index.html

Google Patents
https://patents.google.com/

United States Patent and Trademark Office
https://www.uspto.gov/

World Intellectual Property Organization
https://www.wipo.int/

BLOGS AND WEB RESOURCES

Drug Channels
https://www.drugchannels.com

DrugPatentWatch Blog
https://www.drugpatentwatch.com/blog

DrugWonks
https://drugwonks.com/

FDA Law Blog
http://www.fdalawblog.net/

Orange Book Blog
https://www.orangebookblog.com/

Patent Docs
https://www.patentdocs.org/

Patently-O
https://patentlyo.com/

OTHER BOOKS

ANDA Litigation and Pre-ANDA Litigation, Kenneth L. Dorsney, Editor-in-Chief
Reviews at https://www.drugpatentwatch.com/blog/anda-litigation-strategies-and-tactics-for-pharmaceutical-patent-litigators/ and https://www.drugpatentwatch.com/blog/pre-anda-litigation-strategies-and-tactics-for-developing-a-drug-product-and-patent-portfolio/

Building Biotechnology, Yali Friedman
https://www.BuildingBiotechnology.com

The Generic Challenge, Martin Voet
Review at <https://www.drugpatentwatch.com/blog/the-generic-challenge/

Generic Pharmaceutical Patent and FDA Law, Shashank Upadhye
Review at https://www.drugpatentwatch.com/blog/generic-pharmaceutical-patent-and-fda-law/

Guidelines for the Examination of Patent Applications Relating to Pharmaceuticals
https://www.undp.org/content/dam/undp/library/HIV-AIDS/UNDP_patents_final_web_2.pdf

How to Conduct Patent Searches for Medicines. A Step-by-Step Guide
https://apps.who.int/medicinedocs/documents/s17398e/
s17398e.pdf

www.ingramcontent.com/pod-product-compliance
Lightning Source LLC
Chambersburg PA
CBHW030331220326
41518CB00048B/2234